World of Discovery

Great Cities

Contents

TIME ZONE MAP   **6–7**
INTRODUCTION   **8–9**

DUBLIN, IRELAND, GMT   10
EDINBURGH, SCOTLAND, GMT   12
LONDON, ENGLAND, GMT   14
LISBON, PORTUGAL, GMT   16
MARRAKECH, MOROCCO, GMT   18
CASABLANCA, MOROCCO, GMT   22
MADRID, SPAIN, GMT+1   24
BARCELONA, SPAIN, GMT+1   26
PARIS, FRANCE, GMT+1   28
MONTE CARLO, MONACO, GMT+1   30
BRUGES, BELGIUM, GMT+1   32
BRUSSELS, BELGIUM, GMT+1   34
AMSTERDAM, NETHERLANDS, GMT+1   36
OSLO, NORWAY, GMT+1   38
COPENHAGEN, DENMARK, GMT+1   40
BERLIN, GERMANY, GMT+1   42
MUNICH, GERMANY, GMT+1   44
VENICE, ITALY, GMT+1   46

FLORENCE, ITALY, GMT+1   50
ROME, ITALY, GMT+1   52
PRAGUE, CZECH REPUBLIC, GMT+1   54
LJUBLJANA, SLOVENIA, GMT+1   56
VIENNA, AUSTRIA, GMT+1   58
BRATISLAVA, SLOVAKIA, GMT+1   60
DUBROVNIK, CROATIA, GMT+1   62
BUDAPEST, HUNGARY, GMT+1   66
KRAKOW, POLAND, GMT+1   68
WARSAW, POLAND, GMT+1   70
ATHENS, GREECE, GMT+2   72
ISTANBUL, TURKEY, GMT+2   74
JERUSALEM, ISRAEL, GMT+2   76
CAIRO, EGYPT, GMT+2   80
JOHANNESBURG, SOUTH AFRICA, GMT+2   82
CAPE TOWN, SOUTH AFRICA, GMT+2   84
ST. PETERSBURG, RUSSIA, GMT+3   86
MOSCOW, RUSSIA, GMT+3   88

DUBAI, UNITED ARAB EMIRATES, GMT+4	90
DELHI, INDIA, GMT+5.5	92
KOLKATA, INDIA, GMT+5.5	94
BANGKOK, THAILAND, GMT+7	96
HO CHI MINH CITY, VIETNAM, GMT+7	100
KUALA LUMPUR, MALAYSIA, GMT+8	102
SINGAPORE, SINGAPORE, GMT+8	104
HONG KONG, CHINA, GMT+8	106
SHANGHAI, CHINA, GMT+8	108
BEIJING, CHINA, GMT+8	110
PERTH, AUSTRALIA, GMT+8	112
TOKYO, JAPAN, GMT+9	114
SYDNEY, AUSTRALIA, GMT+10	116
MELBOURNE, AUSTRALIA, GMT+10	120
AUCKLAND, NEW ZEALAND, GMT+12	122
VANCOUVER, CANADA, GMT-8	124
SEATTLE, USA, GMT-8	126
SAN FRANCISCO, USA, GMT-8	128

LOS ANGELES, USA, GMT-8	130
LAS VEGAS, USA, GMT-8	132
MEXICO CITY, MEXICO, GMT-6	134
CHICAGO, USA, GMT-6	136
QUÉBEC, CANADA, GMT-5	138
MONTRÉAL, CANADA, GMT-5	140
TORONTO, CANADA, GMT-5	142
BOSTON, USA, GMT-5	144
NEW YORK, USA, GMT-5	146
WASHINGTON, DC, USA, GMT-5	150
MIAMI, USA, GMT-5	152
HAVANA, CUBA, GMT-5	154
REYKJAVÍK, ICELAND, GMT	156
INDEX	158
ACKNOWLEDGMENTS	160

+1   +2   +3   +4   +5   +6   +7   +8   +9   +10   +11   +12

Time Zone Map

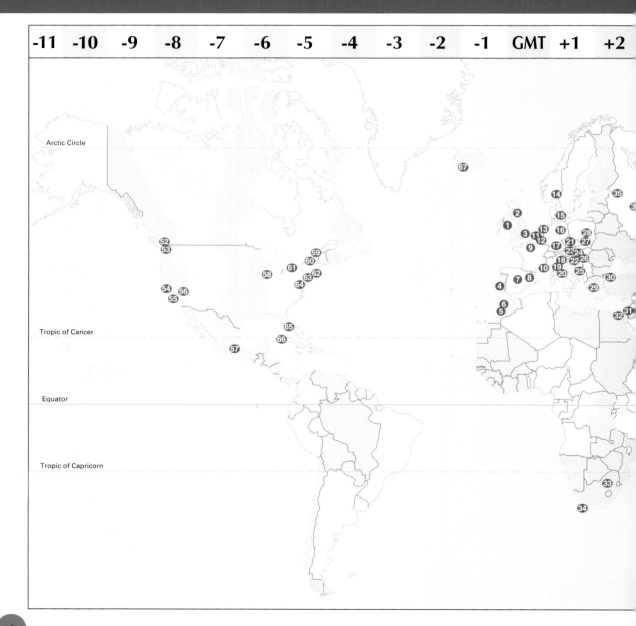

-11	-10	-9	-8	-7	-6	-5	-4	-3	-2	-1	GMT	+1	+2

Arctic Circle

Tropic of Cancer

Equator

Tropic of Capricorn

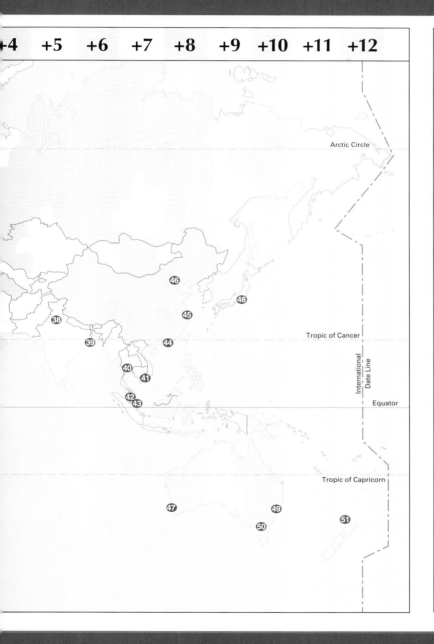

+4 +5 +6 +7 +8 +9 +10 +11 +12

Arctic Circle

Tropic of Cancer

International Date Line

Equator

Tropic of Capricorn

The cities

1	Dublin	35	St. Petersburg
2	Edinburgh	36	Moscow
3	London	37	Dubai
4	Lisbon	38	Delhi
5	Marrakech	39	Kolkata
6	Casablanca	40	Bangkok
7	Madrid	41	Ho Chi Minh City
8	Barcelona	42	Kuala Lumpur
9	Paris	43	Singapore
10	Monte Carlo	44	Hong Kong
11	Bruges	45	Shanghai
12	Brussels	46	Beijing
13	Amsterdam	47	Perth
14	Oslo	48	Tokyo
15	Copenhagen	49	Sydney
16	Berlin	50	Melbourne
17	Munich	51	Auckland
18	Venice	52	Vancouver
19	Florence	53	Seattle
20	Rome	54	San Francisco
21	Prague	55	Los Angeles
22	Ljubljana	56	Las Vegas
23	Vienna	57	Mexico City
24	Bratislava	58	Chicago
25	Dubrovnik	59	Québec
26	Budapest	60	Montréal
27	Krakow	61	Toronto
28	Warsaw	62	Boston
29	Athens	63	New York
30	Istanbul	64	Washington
31	Jerusalem	65	Miami
32	Cairo	66	Havana
33	Johannesburg	67	Rekjavik
34	Cape Town		

What time is it where?

In 1884 the International Meridian Conference divided the world's 360 degrees of longitude into 15-degree time zones, one for each hour of the 24 hour day. As the zero degree line of longitude ran through Greenwich, Great Britain, basic time for the world was established as Greenwich Mean Time or GMT. Time east of Greenwich is ahead of GMT and time west of Greenwich behind.

Zones shown on the map are Standard Time; Summer Time or Daylight Saving Time, adopted by some countries for part of the year, is not shown.

Introduction

Some of our earliest legends and stories revolve around cities—whether as biblical paradoxes reflecting the best or worst of their citizens; communities and powerhouses to be sacked and burned by warrior heroes of the Ancient world; possessions to be built up and fought over as empires shifted and changed through history; as the home of those fictional streets "paved with gold" where sharp-witted migrants from the country could seek (and sometimes find) their fortunes.

The reality is pretty close to the mythology, as you will discover in this revealing exploration of nearly 70 cities from around the world. Indeed, in this modern age cities are still the treasure-houses of their nations, still being fought over in bloody battles from which heroes emerge, and still growing as populations become ever more urbanized.

Within the pages that follow, each city is brought to life through photos and factual information, its location carefully plotted and its distinguishing features disclosed. All the greatest and most revered world capitals are here of course—including Jerusalem, Cairo, Rome, Athens, London, Paris, Berlin, Moscow, Bangkok—and they are set alongside cities that are famous for their presence in other ways—such as Venice, Krakow, Monte Carlo, St. Petersburg, Singapore, Sydney, Los Angeles, Washington, Havana.

Enjoy new angles on the familiar and the surprises of the new as you turn the pages and discover the wonder and fascination of the world's greatest cities.

Dublin

THE CULTURED AND HISTORIC CAPITAL OF THE IRISH REPUBLIC IS KNOWN AS MUCH TODAY FOR ITS VIBRANT NIGHTLIFE AS FOR ITS ELEGANT GEORGIAN STYLE.

north & south

- The city is split in two by the River Liffey.

- Dublin has a dual personality to match, retaining many of its Gaelic names and roots while keeping up with the modern economy of Europe since it joined the EU in 1973.

- The historic heart of the city lies to the south of the river, with many important Georgian buildings and world-class museums.

? Around 48 percent of the population of Dublin is under the age of 35.

Q What is Phoenix Park's claim to fame?

A At 1,728 acres (691ha), it's the biggest city park in Europe.

Eire

history & **story**

- Dublin was founded in Viking times, but only became the capital of the Irish Republic in 1949.

- Dublin has the oldest university in Ireland— Trinity College, which dates back to 1592— as well as two further universities.

- One of Dublin's best-loved claims to fame is as the home of the Guinness Brewery. It was founded in 1759, and it is estimated that around 10 million pints of the black stuff are drunk around the world every year.

- Dublin is known as a party city, with the St. Patrick's Day celebrations alone taking up five days in March (and that's not including recovery time!). The Irish patron saint is feted with fireworks, carnival parades, arts events, and a huge outdoor dance, attracting around 1.2 million people to join in.

Q *What is traditional Irish dancing called?*

A *Set dancing.*

did **you** know?

...it's here?

Edinburgh

SCOTLAND'S CAPITAL, DOMINATED BY ITS CASTLE, IS BUILT ON A SPINE OF VOLCANIC ROCK, WITH AN OLD TOWN DATING TO CELTIC TIMES AND AN 18TH-CENTURY NEW TOWN.

arts &
entertainment

- Edinburgh is the home of the biggest arts festival in the world, which draws millions of visitors each summer.

- The Edinburgh Festival was founded in 1947, with an aim of reuniting the postwar world through the medium of the arts.

- Today it has many sections beyond classical music and theater, including a jazz festival, a book festival, and the famous Tattoo with its military bands and iconic lone piper, a show which is televised around the world.

- A vibrant amateur Fringe festival has grown up too, showcasing up-and-coming comic and theatrical talent, filling every unlikely venue with something unusual, and adding color to the city streets as students do their best to attract an audience to their productions.

literary &
political

- Edinburgh is famous for its cultural roots, as the birthplace or home of great writers including novelists Sir Walter Scott, Robert Louis Stevenson, and Sir Arthur Conan Doyle.

- The Scottish Parliament, re-established in 1999, has given the city Scotland's most striking piece of modern architecture: the new Parliament Building, opened by the Queen in 2004.

did **you** know?

...it's here?

Alba

Q *Which famous buildings stand at the top and bottom of Edinburgh's Royal Mile?*

A *Edinburgh Castle and Holyrood Palace.*

Edinburgh *Scotland*

At midday in Edinburgh it is 8am in San Juan and 6am in Mexico City…   *…do you know where they are?*

13

London

Q Which national hero stands atop a pillar in the middle of Trafalgar Square?

A Admiral Lord Nelson.

historical & **happening**

- London has been scarred by a series of major catastrophes, starting with the Great Plague of 1665 which killed up to 100,000 citizens.

- In 1666 the Great Fire of London destroyed around 80 percent of the city's buildings, an event recorded at first hand by the great diarist Samuel Pepys (1633–1703).

- Devastation came again in 1940, when 30,000 people died and more than 30 percent of the city was wrecked by German bombs during the period known as the Blitz.

- London's newest attraction is the 444ft (135m) Millennium Wheel on the south bank of the River Thames, which carries visitors high above the city for outstanding views. Other top attractions include the Tower of London, St. Paul's Cathedral, and Buckingham Palace.

did **you** know?

...it's here?

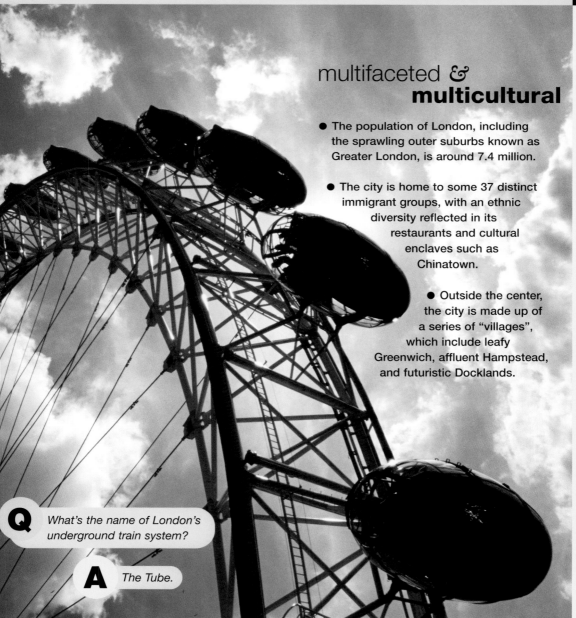

multifaceted &
multicultural

● The population of London, including the sprawling outer suburbs known as Greater London, is around 7.4 million.

● The city is home to some 37 distinct immigrant groups, with an ethnic diversity reflected in its restaurants and cultural enclaves such as Chinatown.

● Outside the center, the city is made up of a series of "villages", which include leafy Greenwich, affluent Hampstead, and futuristic Docklands.

Q *What's the name of London's underground train system?*

A The Tube.

At midday in London it is 2pm in Johannesburg and 8am in Santiago…   *…do you know where they are?*

Lisbon

ancient & modern

- The heart of this lovely old city is characterized by its creaking trams and funiculars, its cobbled streets, and elegant 18th-century buildings.

- The suburb of Belém has some of the best old buildings, including the monastery of Jerónimos, built in 1502 to give thanks for New World riches.

- The waterfront area was redeveloped for the 1998 Lisbon Expo, including some stunning modern architecture in the Parc des Nacoes area, such as the palm-like structure of the Oriente train station.

- The sweeping lines of the ultramodern Vasco da Gama suspension bridge cross the River Tagus.

Lisbon *Portugal*

renaissance &
energy

- Lisbon's first great come-back was after the devastation of a massive earthquake in 1755, when the city was rebuilt to a grid pattern.

- Its second was at the end of the 20th century, when access to funding via the European Union gave it a new injection of energy and a chance to rebuild and redevelop on a grand scale.

Q *What is the name of Lisbon's biggest public park?*

A *Parque Eduardo VI.*

? The Romans established their provincial capital of Olissipo on the site of present-day Lisbon in 138BC.

did **you** know?

...it's here?

Marrakech

Morocco

المملكة المغربية

WITH A STARTLING BACKDROP OF SNOW-CAPPED MOUNTAINS, MARRAKECH IS AN EXOTIC CITY, AND ONE OF THE MOST EXCITING DESTINATIONS IN NORTH AFRICA.

 TIME ZONE: MARRAKECH GMT

Marrakech *Morocco*

Q When did Morocco gain independence from France?

A In 1956.

19

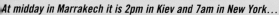

At midday in Marrakech it is 2pm in Kiev and 7am in New York...   *...do you know where they are?*

Q Which famous wartime prime minister of Britain came to Marrakech to paint?

A Winston Churchill.

facts &
figures

- Marrakech is the capital of Morocco, a country that was once a protectorate of France, and is now an independent kingdom ruled by Mohammed VI.

- The city was founded in 1062, and now has a population of 848,000, with Berbers and Arabs making up the largest groups.

souks &
markets

- Various *souks* (markets) lie within the old city (Médina), and you can buy anything from lizards and spices to carpets.

- The most famous market is held on the Djemma El Fna square. It has been described as the greatest circus on earth, with storytellers and acrobats.

did **you** know?

...it's here?

Casablanca

Developed around one of the largest artificial ports in the world, the busy industrial "white house" city has a distinctly European feel to it.

TIME ZONE: CASABLANCA GMT

المملكة المغربية

highlights &
superlatives

- With a population of almost 4 million, Casablanca is the largest port in northwest Africa and the biggest metropolis in Morocco.

- The beautiful white Mosque of Hassan II is the second biggest in the world, and its minaret, at 688ft (210m), is the tallest in the world.

- The Marché Central, built and named by the French, is the biggest fruit and vegetable market in Morocco.

modern &
thriving

- New by North African standards, Casablanca was built out of the remains of a pirate haven and named by the Portuguese in 1515. It was rebuilt in 1757 after a major earthquake.

- Casablanca is a working city, with industries that include fishing, fish-canning, saw-milling, furniture, construction materials, glass, textiles, electronic goods, leather, processed food, beer, spirits, soft drinks, and cigarettes.

- Top sporting facilities around the city include a racing circuit for Formula One cars at Ain Diab, and a world-class golf course to the north.

did **you** know?

...it's here?

Madrid

THE SPANISH CAPITAL, SET ON THE HIGH PLATEAU IN THE MIDDLE OF THE IBERIAN PENINSULA, OFFERS A RICH MIXTURE OF HIGH CULTURE AND HIGH-OCTANE PARTYING.

culture &
nightlife

- The Spanish royal court was first established in Madrid in 1561, and many of the city's most gracious buildings, boulevards, and fountains date from the 18th century.

- The city boasts three great museums: the Prado, the Thyssen-Bornemisza, and the Reina Sofia (modern art in a striking glass tower).

- Chic shopping is a pleasure in Madrid, but for life at all levels go for the chaos and fun of the famous Rastro flea market.

- Late-night partying is part of the city's culture, with the so-called *madrugada* coming to life between the hours of midnight and 6am. Don't think of dining before 10pm, and anticipate traffic problems at 4am as the bright young things block the streets, heading for home or moving on to early-morning discos or clubs.

Q *In which year was the monarchy restored to power in Spain?*

A *1975, on the death of General Franco.*

did **you** know?

...it's here?

España

bulls &
toreadors

- Madrid's Plaza de Toros is the most important bullring in the world, and seats up to 22,000 spectators passionate for the *corrida* (fight).

- The bullring was built in 1934 and is a temple to the bullfighter's art, imitating Moorish and Christian architecture of the 13th and 14th centuries.

 Q *What mantle did Madrid take on in 1992?*

 A *European City of Culture.*

At midday in Madrid it is 6am in Ottawa and 3am in San Francisco...   *...do you know where they are?*

Barcelona

? Today Barcelona's status is restored as the capital of Catalunya, an autonomous region within the country of Spain.

Q Who sang the theme song to the Barcelona Olympics in 1992?

A Freddie Mercury

España

history &
conflict

- Barcelona was founded by the Romans around a natural harbor in 15BC, and parts of its Roman walls still stand today.

- In AD988 Barcelona became the flourishing capital of the independent state of Catalunya, and only bowed reluctantly to Spanish rule in the early 15th century.

- With a prosperity gained largely from the textile industry, the city took an anti-nationalist stand in the Spanish Civil War (1936–39). When it finally fell to Franco, it found that its Catalan language, identity, and culture were supressed.

architecture &
style

- Barcelona has become synonymous with the works of architect Antonio Gaudí (1852–1926). His unique Modernist style can be seen all over the city, from chimneypots to mosaics.

- Gaudí's most famous building is the Sagrada Família cathedral, unfinished at his death and still incomplete today.

- Look for his vibrant mosaics of colored, broken ceramic tiles in the green outdoor space of the Parc Güell. They encrust statues and sinuous buildings alike, and have been much imitated around the world.

did **you** know?

...it's here?

At midday in Barcelona it is 7pm in Shanghai and 2pm in Nairobi...   *...do you know where they are?*

Paris

THE GRAND OLD LADY OF FRANCE, PARIS IS A BYWORD FOR STYLE AND ROMANCE THAT HAS REINVENTED ITSELF ARCHITECTURALLY FOR THE 21ST CENTURY.

landmarks &
highlights

- The Louvre is the biggest museum in the world, covering more than 1.7 million square feet (153,000sq m), and houses the most famous portrait in the world: Leonardo da Vinci's enigmatic *Mona Lisa*.

- The Eiffel Tower was built in 1889 as the centerpiece of an exhibition-cum-trade fair. You can climb the 1,665 steps for a view over the city.

- The Arc de Triomphe stands on a traffic island on the broad Champs Élysées avenue, marking battles won by national hero Napoleon Bonaparte (1769–1821).

La France

Q The storming of the Bastille prison in 1789 marked what great event?

A The start of the French Revolution.

style &
haute couture

- Architecture reflects Parisian self-confidence and style, from the spectacular Arche de la Défense to the art nouveau swirls of the Métro.

- The Parisians invented chic, of course, and you can see it at the festival of high style that is Paris Fashion Week.

did **you** know?

...it's here?

At midday in Paris it is 6am in Boston and 8pm in Rio de Janeiro...   *...do you know where they are?*

Monte Carlo

THIS MODERN HIGH-RISE CITY IS CROWDED INTO THE TINY PRINCIPALITY OF MONACO, WITH AN UNRIVALED REPUTATION FOR FAST MONEY, FAST CARS, AND FAST LIVING.

Q Which neighbor has threatened Monaco's independence over the centuries?

A France (Spain and Sardinia have also laid claim).

did **you** know?

...it's here?

Principauté de Monaco

glitzy &
glamorous

- Monte Carlo's most famous building is not some historic palace or cathedral, but its lavish Casino, which first opened its doors in 1863.

- The city first shut down its streets to host a Grand Prix motor race in 1929, and it's been a firm favorite on the racing circuit ever since.

- Famous names linked with Monte Carlo include Mata Hari, the dancer and spy, who shot another spy dead inside the Casino; and movie stars Richard Burton and Elizabeth Taylor.

tax-free &
crime-free

- Citizens of Monaco pay no income tax, something that has attracted hundreds of the rich and famous to seek sanctuary here. It's not surprising, therefore, that real estate in Monte Carlo is at a premium few in the world can afford.

- The city has the highest concentration of police per square foot in the world, meaning it is virtually crime-free.

Q *Which movie star married into the Grimaldi royal family?*

A *Grace Kelly, who married Prince Rainier in 1956.*

Bruges

medieval &
beautiful

- Bruges, a medieval gem on the broad plain of Flanders, was once a wealthy trading center linked to the North Sea by canals, and capital of the state of Burgundy.

- The wide square known as the Markt (market) was the hub. Today it's surrounded by elegant, gabled guildhalls that mostly house appealing restaurants and cafés, where you can sit out on the sidewalk and watch the world go by.

- The city's most visible landmark is the belfry tower of Belfort, which dates back to the 13th century. It has a carillon of 47 bells which ring out tunefully over the old quarter.

- Narrow cobbled streets and peaceful waterways radiate from the center to an outer, encircling canal that reflects the oval shape of the now-vanished city walls.

did **you** know?

...it's here?

Belgique

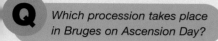

Q *Which procession takes place in Bruges on Ascension Day?*

A *The Holy Blood Procession, dating back to 1291.*

chocolate & **lace**

- Belgium is famed for its hand-made chocolate. It is one of the delights of Bruges, decorating the shop windows and scenting the air.

- Lace-making was first practised here during the Middle Ages. Its history is traced in two fine museums, and the fine lace is still sold today. Designs often reflect local scenes and flowers.

33

Brussels

political &
powerful

- The capital of Belgium since 1830, Brussels made the shift from a provincial capital to a world-class city towards the end of the 20th century.

- As the home of the European Commission, the European Parliament, and the Council of Europe, Brussels now jealously guards its status as the unofficial "capital" of Europe.

- This is where European Union members must look to for EU subsidies, rules and regulations, judgements, and bureaucratic procedures.

- In addition to being the capital of Belgium, Brussels is also the capital of Belgium's Dutch-speaking region of Flanders—but there are still many more people in the city who speak French as their first language.

Q *Who was defeated at the Battle of Waterloo, just outside Brussels, in 1815?*

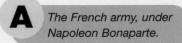

A *The French army, under Napoleon Bonaparte.*

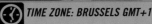

Belgique

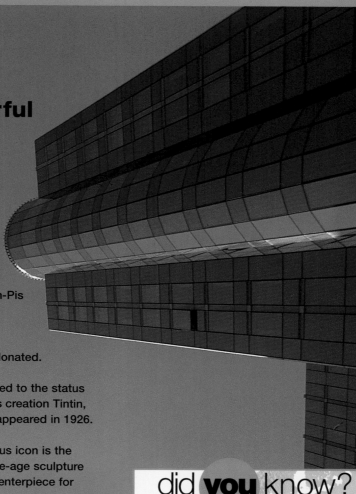

cosmopolitan &
colorful

- Its location on the border between Germanic northern Europe and the Latin south means that both the French and Dutch languages are widely spoken here.

- The city's most famous icon is a bronze fountain statue which depicts a small boy urinating. The Manneken-Pis is so well loved at home and abroad that he has his own wardrobe of more than 750 outfits, specially made and donated.

- Comic books have been raised to the status of art here, thanks to Hergé's creation Tintin, the boy detective, who first appeared in 1926.

- Brussels' second most famous icon is the weird Atomium, a huge space-age sculpture of an iron crystal built as a centerpiece for the World Fair of 1958.

- In the restaurants and beer-cellars of Brussels you can sample around 450 different Belgian beers—which provide the perfect accompaniment to the hearty local food.

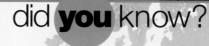

did **you** know?

...it's here?

Amsterdam

THE LOW-LYING CAPITAL OF THE NETHERLANDS (ALSO KNOWN AS HOLLAND), FAMED FOR
ITS HIGH-GABLED, NARROW HOUSES BUILT ON A NETWORK OF CANALS.

old masters &
a troubled history

- The Rijksmuseum holds the national collection of Dutch Old Masters, including paintings by the great artists Rembrandt (1606–1669) and Vermeer (1632–75). Don't miss Rembrandt's restored masterpiece *The Night Watch*.

- The house where teenager Anne Frank hid from the Nazis with her family between 1942 and 1944, in silence and fear is now an evocative museum. Their sanctuary betrayed, this Jewish family were sent to concentration camps, where Anne died in 1945, age 15, but her spirit lives on in her remarkable diary.

- The Van Gogh Museum is an outstanding art gallery dedicated to the work of the artist Vincent Van Gogh. It showcases an unrivaled collection of his paintings from every stage of his life, including the famous *Sunflowers*.

trade &
tourism

- It's been the Dutch capital since 1814—but not the seat of government.

- The lowest point in the Dutch capital lies 18ft (5.5m) below sea level.

- Commercial trade here is based on tourism, diamonds, cheese, plants, and flowers.

did **you** know?

...it's here?

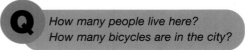

Q *How many people live here?*
How many bicycles are in the city?

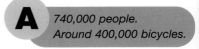

A *740,000 people.*
Around 400,000 bicycles.

Q What is this tower, and who is buried here?

A The Westerkerk tower, begun in 1619 by Hendrick de Keyset and consecrated in 1631. Rembrandt is buried in the graveyard.

At midday in Amsterdam it is 4.45pm in Kathmandu and 6pm in Bangkok…   *…do you know where they are?*

Oslo

plague &
recovery

- At only just over half a million, Oslo's population today is not exactly big for a capital city—but that's still about 12 percent of the population of the whole country.

- In 1350 the population of Oslo was slashed, when around two-thirds died in a terrible outbreak of bubonic plague. Power shifted to Copenhagen in Denmark.

- By the 19th century the city was recovering economically, and at this time became a flourishing center for art and literature.

- The discovery of oil in the 1970s completed the transformation.

did **you** know?

...it's here?

Norge

art &
architecture

● Outdoor modern art is everywhere in the city, most famously in the sturdy statues of people who fill Frognor Park.

● Norwegian painter Edvard Munch was one of many artists attracted to live in the city, and he has his own dedicated museum here, including his most famous work, *The Scream* (1893).

● The city was founded in 1048 by Harald Hårdråda, at the top of a dramatic 70-mile (112km) long fjord in the southeast of the country. Today one of the oldest buildings is the Akerhus Slott (castle), which dates back to 1300.

● The 1950s redbrick Rådhus (town hall) is where the prestigious Nobel Peace Prize is awarded at the end of each year.

Q *Which famous Norwegian explorer, whose ship* Fram *is in Oslo, was the first man to reach the South Pole?*

A *Roald Amundsen, in December 1911.*

? From November to February, the average daily temperature in Oslo is below freezing point.

Copenhagen

SCANDINAVIA'S LARGEST CITY OWES ITS PROSPERITY AND STYLISH ELEGANCE TO LONG PERIODS OF ECONOMIC AND POLITICAL STABILITY.

waterways & **culture**

- A boat-borne tour of Copenhagen's canals and rivers reveals the scale of the network of waterway in this expansive and beautiful Baltic city, once a major trading port.

- The building of the Øresund Bridge has finally given the city a permanent link to its Baltic neighbor, Sweden, helping to elevate its importance within Scandinavia, and to link that region with the rest of Europe.

- Copenhagen is known for its theaters and brand-new opera house, its world-class museums, and its cutting-edge modern design (especially of furniture and jewelry).

fairy-tale & **romance**

- Hans Christian Andersen (1805–75) wrote more than 350 folk tales which still delight children worldwide. His best-known story is that of *The Ugly Duckling* who turned into a swan.

- His best-loved monument is the statue of the *Little Mermaid*, perched wistfully on a rock by the shore in the Øresund Sound.

Q *Which American star played Hans Christian Andersen in a 1952 musical biopic?*

A *Danny Kaye.*

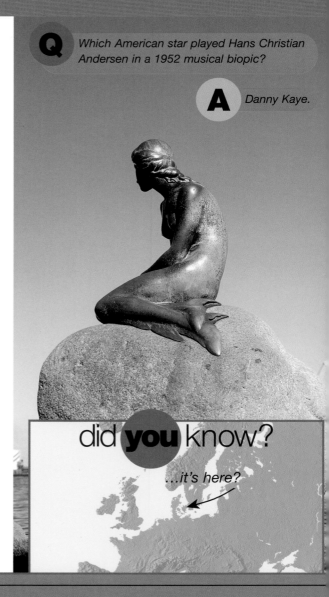

did **you** know?

...it's here?

Danmark

Denmark

? Copenhagen's central Tivoli Gardens are a pleasure garden and theme park covering a total area of 3.2 square miles (8.3sq km).

At midday in Copenhagen it is 7pm in Perth and 1pm in Beirut...   *...do you know where they are?*

Berlin

THE REJUVENATED CAPITAL OF GERMANY, BERLIN IS THE POLITICAL, FINANCIAL, AND CULTURAL HEART OF A REUNITED NATION.

Q What building is this and which famous British architect designed it?

A This is the glass dome of the Reichstag, built between 1992 and 1999, which was designed by Sir Norman Foster.

Q Why is this church (right) an iconic symbol of Berlin?

A The Kaiser-Wilhelm-Gedächtniskirche is a monument in Berlin after being damaged during the bombing raids of World War II.

reunification &
olympic glory

- Berlin impressed the world with its lavish staging of the Olympic Games in 1936.

- The city was crudely divided by a wall in 1961, to separate the Communist East from the decadent West.

- The city was reunited when the wall was finally torn down in 1989.

- Berlin has a population of 3.4 million (the population of Germany is 82.5 million).

landmarks &
nicknames

- The Reichstag is Germany's 19th-century parliament building. It has a spectacular modern glass dome designed by English architect Sir Norman Foster.

- The Tiergarten is a vast park in the middle of the city, leading up to the famous Brandenburg Gate.

- The stark ruin of the Kaiser Wilhelm Memorial Church (known in German as Kaiser-Wilhelm-Gedächtniskirche), is on the exclusive shopping street of Kurfürstenstrasse. Standing beside the modern steel and glass church tower, it is a reminder of the city's wartime history.

- Energetic, witty, and irreverent, Berliners delight in pricking any pomposity, and every monument in the city has its own nickname: the Memorial Church is the "Hollow Tooth," and the boxy modern Chancellery is the "Washing Machine."

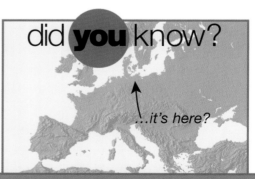

did **you** know?

...it's here?

Munich

It is said that, given the choice, more than half the population of Germany would choose to live in this gracious old city, famous for its beer.

Q Which famous composer became Kappellmeister (musical director) in the city in 1894?

A Richard Strauss.

Deutschland

industry &
brewing

- Munich is the economic heart of Germany, and international giants such as BMW and Siemens have their headquarters here.

- It is best known, however, for the production, consumption, and celebration of beer, with no fewer than six main breweries in the city.

- Its citizens consume an average of 42 gallons (190 liters) of beer each per year, in the beer halls and beer cellars that can be found all over the city. The beer garden in the Englischer Garten, can seat over 7,000 drinkers at a time.

- It's not surprising, then, that Munich holds the biggest beer festival in the world—the two-week long Oktoberfest. It takes place in September, drawing 7 million visitors.

history &
architecture

- Munich suffered devastation from bombing during World War II, and was largely rebuilt in the years that followed.

- The symbol of Munich is the Italianate twin onion-domes that top the towers of the cathedral, the Frauenkirche.

did **you** know?

...it's here?

At midday in Munich it is 3pm in Abu Dhabi and 5am in New Orleans...   *...do you know where they are?*

Venice

Italia

Italy

VENICE IS UNDOUBTEDLY ONE OF THE MOST ROMANTIC CITIES IN THE WORLD, WITH ITS BEAUTIFUL OLD PALACES AND CHURCHES, ITS WATERWAYS AND BRIDGES.

monuments &
landmarks

- The Doge's Palace and the Basilica of St. Mark are significant city landmarks, dating from the 9th century, which front on to the open space of piazza San Marco.

- The outlying island of Murano is known for the quality and variety of its hand-blown glass, which reflects modern and historic designs.

carnevale &
partying

- The Venice Carnival (or *Carnevale*) reached its height in the heady excesses of the 16th, 17th, and 18th centuries.

- Carnevale was revived in the 1980s, and is celebrated with colorful costumes and masks, balls and entertainments, in the days leading up to Lent.

bridges &
canals

- Venice was built on a cluster of more than 100 small islands in a salt-water lagoon, protected from the sea by the islands of the Lido and Pellestrina, and is subject to tidal rise and fall.

- Its most famous water-highway is the Grand Canal, stretching for 2.5 miles (4km) and lined with palatial mansions and churches.

- High-prowed, black water-taxis known as gondolas are rowed by a single oar up and down the main waterways by gondoliers, who are traditionally dressed in straw hats and may sing to their customers (for an extra fee).

- The dozens of smaller canals are crossed by about 400 bridges, of which the most recognizable is the high-backed Rialto.

did **you** know?

...it's here?

Q Where in the world can you see an indoor re-creation of Venice, complete with singing gondoliers?

A The Venetian Hotel, Las Vegas.

Venice *Italy*

49

Florence

More than 2 million visitors a year crowd into the ancient heart of this fascinating old city to admire its outstanding art collections.

power &
architecture

- Founded by the Romans, Florence became a free city state in the 12th century, with its own ruling assembly and a thriving economy based on banking and trade.

- For a short time at the end of the 19th century the city became the capital of the newly united Italy, and it is still the capital of Tuscany.

- Florence's most remarkable building is the *duomo*, or cathedral, dedicated to Santa Maria del Fiore. It is topped by a vast orange-tiled dome, the largest in the world, an innovation designed in the 15th century by the Tuscan architect Brunelleschi.

- The Ponte Vecchio is another extraordinary feature—an old bridge over the River Arno, with a superstructure of houses and shops.

did **you** know?

...it's here?

? Michelangelo's statue of David, in the Galleria dell'Accademia, was designed proportionately to be admired from below.

Medici &
magnificent

- The powerful and ultra-wealthy Medici family controlled Florence through the Renaissance period, from 1458 to 1743.

- Under their patronage, artists, architects, and sculptors flourished, and their legacy can be seen in the Uffizi gallery.

- Lorenzo the Magnificent, himself a poet of some skill, was head of the dynasty—and the city—from 1469 to 1492. He is remembered today for his patronage of great artists such as Botticelli and Michelangelo.

Florence *Italy*

Q *How many museums are in the Medici palace, the Palazzo Pitti, alone?*

A Five.

Rome

ONCE ROME LAY AT THE CENTER OF A GREAT EMPIRE. TODAY IT IS A BUSTLING SURVIVOR, WITH TRAFFIC RUNNING CONSTANTLY ROUND ITS ANCIENT STRUCTURES.

Q *Which tiny independent state within Rome issues its own postage stamps?*

A *The Vatican State, founded in 1929.*

venerable & **venerated**

● According to legend, Rome was founded by the twins Romulus and Remus, who as orphaned babies were suckled by a she-wolf.

● The city was founded in the eighth century BC and quickly grew to be a major power, and the heart of the Roman Empire. The Colosseum is the most visible remnant of this time, but the city is littered with other Roman sites.

● In AD590 Pope Gregory I established Rome as the papal seat. The wealth this brought built classical structures such as St. Peter's Basilica.

● The millennium celebration for 2000 marked the end of a massive restoration and refurbishment program across the city.

? Rome's finest alleyways, palaces, and fountain-filled piazzas are in the city's historic center.

did **you** know?

...it's here?

Italia

At midday in Rome it is 8am in Brasília and 6am in Montréal…

...do you know where they are?

Prague

STRADDLING THE BROAD, SHALLOW RIVER VLTAVA, THE GOLDEN-STONED CAPITAL OF THE CZECH REPUBLIC IS ONE OF THE MOST BEAUTIFUL IN EUROPE.

Q *When did the Communist regime of Czechoslovakia finally crumble?*

A *1989, the year of the "Velvet Revolution."*

TIME ZONE: PRAGUE GMT+1

Česká republika

history & **astrology**

- Prague owes much of its character to the 14th-century Emperor Charles IV, who began the Gothic St. Vitus cathedral, bridged the river, and laid out the medieval New Town, which centers on Wenceslas Square.

- The elegant stone Charles Bridge is named after this founding father.

- Medieval beer cellars in the city are still hugely popular with locals and visitors alike.

- Many of Prague's most gracious, Germanic buildings date from the 17th century, when prosperity returned after the Thirty Years War.

- One of the city's best-loved features is the extraordinary gilded astrological clock, which is built onto the side of the town hall overlooking the outdoor cafés of Old Town Square.

culture & **fame**

- The city's beauty has led to Prague featuring as the backdrop in several major international movies, including the James Bond movie *The Living Daylights*.

- The Christmas carol Good King Wenceslas refers to a real Bohemian prince who was murdered by his pagan brother in AD929. He was part of the Premslid dynasty, which founded Prague in the 9th century.

- Wolfgang Amadeus Mozart's acclaimed opera *Don Giovanni* received its premiere in Prague in 1787.

did **you** know?

...it's here?

Ljubljana

THIS COMPACT, APPEALING OLD CITY FOUND ITSELF AT THE HEART OF A POLITICAL STORM IN 1991, WHEN THE REPUBLIC OF SLOVENIA DECLARED ITS INDEPENDENCE.

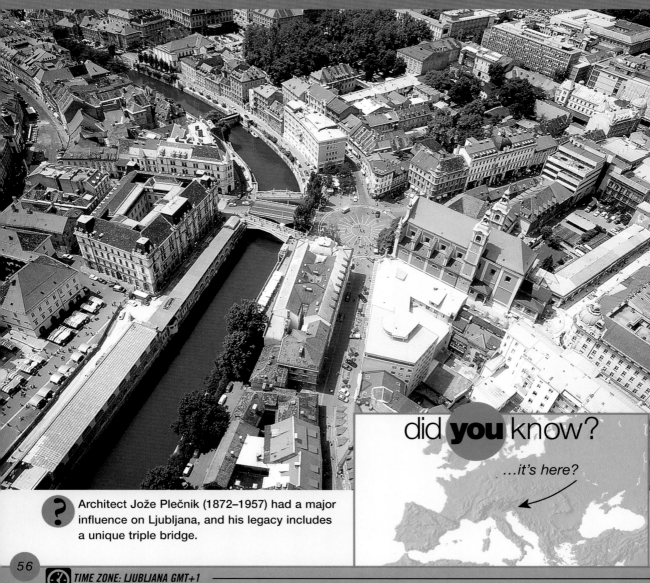

did you know?

...it's here?

? Architect Jože Plečnik (1872–1957) had a major influence on Ljubljana, and his legacy includes a unique triple bridge.

Ljubljana *Slovenia*

facts &
statistics

- Ljubljana's medieval core lies on both banks of the narrow Ljubljanca River.

- Serious earthquakes in 1511 and 1895 demolished large areas of the city, causing widespread devastation.

- Today the city is overlooked by the high walls of Ljubljana Castle, perched on a hilltop. The castle is at the center of much cultural life here, with a Virtual Museum of Ljubljana's history, and it even doubles as a wedding venue.

- Key industries include retail, financial services, and tourism. Around 20 percent of the residents are enrolled at the university, giving the city a predominantly youthful population.

poetry &
culture

- The enthusiastic composing of poetry here has been described as a "national affliction."

- There's even a national holiday dedicated to culture, celebrated on 8 February in memory of the author, France Prešeren (1800–49).

At midday in Ljubljana it is 4pm in Lahore and 3am in Vancouver…   *…do you know where they are?*

Vienna

THE AUSTRIAN CAPITAL IS CHARACTERIZED BY AN OPENNESS AND ELEGANCE THAT OWES MUCH TO ITS DEVELOPMENT UNDER THE INFLUENCE OF EMPEROR FRANZ-JOSEF.

architecture & **elegance**

- It was Franz-Josef (1830–1916) who ordered that the bastions around the edge of the city be torn down and replaced with the Ringstrasse of monumental civic buildings in historicist style.

- Vienna was the capital of the Habsburg Empire from 1278 until its demise in 1918.

- Today Romanesque, Gothic, and Baroque buildings rub shoulders harmoniously with the neo-Gothic city hall, neo-Renaissance museums, luxury apartment blocks, and the university.

- The Hofburg is the mighty, domed palace that was home to the Habsburg rulers, including the formidable Maria Theresa (1717–80).

- Perhaps the nicest way to tour the city is in an open horse-drawn carriage.

did **you** know?

...it's here?

? Mozart wrote some of his best loved pieces during his time in Vienna, including the serenade *Eine kleine Nachtmusik* and the operas *Cosi fan Tutte* and *Die Zauberflöte* (The Magic Flute).

Österreich

Austria

magical &
musical

- Vienna is the home of the Viennese Waltz, and Johann Strauss (the Younger), born here in 1825, composed more than 400 waltzes, including the *Blue Danube* and *Tales from the Vienna Woods*.

- The composer Wolfgang Amadeus Mozart (1756–91) spent only the last ten years of his life in Vienna, but he has become the city's greatest hero.

- Mozart sought and eventually gained a post at the court of the Emperor Joseph II, who ungratefully complained that his opera *Die Entführung aus dem Seraglio* simply contained too many notes.

Q *Which additional title did Emperor Franz Josef adopt in 1867?*

A King of Hungary.

Bratislava

Set on the River Danube, just 38 miles (61km) from Vienna, Bratislava is the capital of Slovakia and a world apart.

history &
politics

- Its central location within Europe means that Bratislava has been occupied at different times by Celts, Romans, Slavs, and French, and it has also been part of Hungary, a short-lived Slovak State, and Czechoslovakia.

- Today it is the most important port on the River Danube, and by far the largest city in Slovakia.

- Its exquisite and immaculately restored Old Town lies in the shadow of Castle Hill, a strategic point whose importance was first recognized during the ninth century.

- The ocher walls of Bratislava Castle stand on a rocky outcrop, part of the Little Carpathian Mountains which fall within the city boundaries.

Q *What modern structure in Bratislava resembles a UFO?*

A *The futuristic New Bridge, topped by a restaurant.*

Slovensko

Bratislava *Slovakia*

population & **housing**

- The population of Bratislava stands at just under half a million.

- Around a quarter of the people live in the suburb of Petržalka, in what is claimed to be the biggest housing estate in Europe. Pre-fabricated multistory apartment blocks stretch from the river almost to the Austrian border, in a project that began under Communist rule in 1976.

did **you** know?

...it's here?

At midday in Bratislava it is 11am in Reykjavík and 8am in São Paulo...   *...do you know where they are?*

Dubrovnik

Hrvatska

Croatia

Dubrovnik's appealing location and beautiful harbor setting have made it an attractive prize for different European powers over the centuries.

Q *A statue of which person stands proudly in Gundulic Square?*

A *Dubrovnik-born poet Ivan Gundulic (1589–1638).*

At midday in Dubrovnik it is 6am in Washington DC, and 7pm in Beijing…   *…do you know where they are?*

did **you** know?

...it's here?

Q Dubrovnik sits on a group of islands. How many?

A 118 in total.

harmony &
history

- Local people have affectionately nicknamed their city "*skladna*." In Croatian the term refers to harmony, a perfect name for a city in perfect harmony with its surroundings.

- Another nickname is the "Pearl of the Adriatic", which refers to its superb coastal location and the beauty of its compact heart.

- The medieval walls of this fortified city have never been breached by an invading army. However, Dubrovnik took a severe battering after Croatia's declaration of independence in 1991, when it was besieged and shelled by Serbian and then Montenegran troops.

- From 1526 to 1806 Dubrovnik was an independent republic, but at other times it has come under the rule of Byzantines, Venetians, Austrians, French, Italians, and Germans.

- Many of the ancient buildings of the Old Town, centered around the lively harbor, date from a rebuild in the 17th century.

festival &
spirit

- Every summer, in July and August, Dubrovnik fills with performers and spectators for an annual festival to celebrate the city's independence and freedom. The festival is known to local people as *Libertas*—liberty.

- The festival dates back to the 16th century, but has only operated in its present form since 1949 (when, post-World War II, the city was part of the now-dissolved Yugoslavia).

- So important is the festival to local spirit that it even went ahead during the siege of the 1990s, with brave actors performing against the very real backdrop of war.

- The festival attracts top performers from around the world, with outdoor spaces transformed into open-air venues, and historic venues that are usually closed to visitors opening their doors.

Budapest

HOME TO ABOUT ONE-FIFTH OF THE TOTAL POPULATION OF HUNGARY, BUDAPEST IS A CITY THAT HAS REVIVED AFTER THE HARDSHIPS OF COMMUNIST RULE.

unity & **freedom**

- A unified Budapest, spread on both banks of the River Danube, has only existed since 1873, when Pest, Óbuda, and Buda were at last formally joined into one metropolis.

- Buda and Pest were known as spa settlements to the Celtic tribes, long before the Romans first tried to link them under the name of Aquincum ("abundant waters").

- Prosperity was destroyed during the two world wars, but in 1989 the city regained its freedom, and now flourishes.

 The huge island in the Danube that stretches downstream is Csepel Island, which became a center of heavy industry in the 19th century.

Magyarország

innovation &
architecture

- Budapest's top sites include the Fisherman's Bastion, the Royal Palace (now the National Gallery), and monumental Hösök tere (Heroes Square) at the end of Andrássy út boulevard.

- The Chain Bridge, built in 1848, was the first permanent stone bridge to be built across the Danube within Hungary.

- The bridge was designed on the instructions of Count István Széchenyi, who also founded Budapest's Academy of Sciences, the National Theater, and the Danube Steam Ship Company.

did **you** know?

...it's here?

At midday in Budapest it is 2pm in Baghdad and 6am in Toronto...

...do you know where they are?

Krakow

WHILE WARSAW IS THE POLITICAL AND ECONOMIC CENTER OF POLAND, THE OLD CITY OF KRAKOW IS VERY MUCH ITS CULTURAL AND SPIRITUAL HEART.

cosmopolitan &
cultured

● Krakow lies to the south of Poland, and its thriving modern economy is based on steel commerce, services, and tourism.

● The city served as the capital of Poland from 1380 to 1596, and today can boast proudly of its legacy of 331 ancient houses, more than 50 churches, and more than 30 museums (which house an estimated 2 million works of art).

● Krakow's magnificent cathedral is the burial place of 41 of Poland's 45 kings, alongside poets and national heroes. It stands adjacent to the Royal Castle, overlooking the Wisla River.

● The Rynek Glówny is the extensive medieval market square in the middle of the exquisite Old Town, surrounded by fascinating buildings including the Italianate Sukiennice (Cloth Hall).

did **you** know?

...it's here?

TIME ZONE: KRAKOW GMT+1

Polska

Poland

papacy &
fame

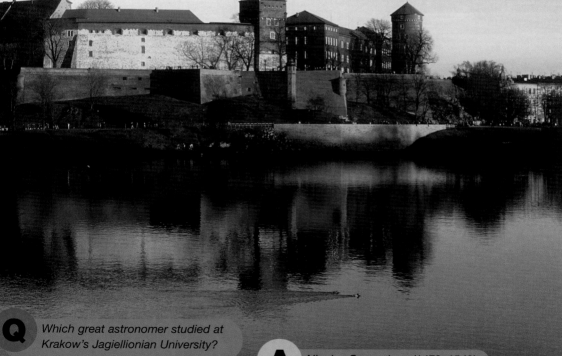

- Krakow's most famous son is Karol Jozef Wojtyla (1920–2005), who served as archbishop here before becoming one of the most powerful men in the world.

- Elected to the papacy in 1978, he took the name Pope John Paul II. He traveled widely, visiting more than 100 countries to promote the messages of tolerance and world peace.

Q *Which great astronomer studied at Krakow's Jagiellionian University?*

 A *Nicolas Copernicus (1473–1543).*

Warsaw

Set on a flat plain near the middle of Poland, Warsaw is a great city that has been beaten many times but never bowed.

? The composer Frédéric Chopin (1810–1849) was born nearby, and his music is celebrated across the city. Between 1826 and 1829 he studied at the Conservatory here.

TIME ZONE: WARSAW GMT+1

Poland

Polska

reconstructed &
prospering

- The reconstruction of Warsaw's mellow Old Town is one of the more surprising legacies of the Communist era, and earned a place on the UNESCO World Heritage List in 1980.

- Some of the most appealing restored buildings cluster round Castle Square, with St. John's Cathedral nearby.

- One of Warsaw's most striking buildings is the brutalist, neo-Gothic Palace of Culture, a "gift" from Joseph Stalin that looms 758ft (231m) over the city. It's now the focus for international trade fairs and exhibitions.

remarkable &
resilient

- Warsaw witnessed some of the most terrible events of World War II, which resulted in the destruction of about 85 percent of its buildings, and the loss of most of its population through death, deportation or transportation to the concentration camps.

- The infamous Warsaw Uprising began on 19 April 1943, when Nazi troops of occupation were ordered to exterminate the city's Jewish population.

- The citizens bravely took a stand and fought back, hiding in the city's ghettos until they were starved out or exterminated.

- The event is commemorated in a poignant Monument to the Ghetto Heroes, erected in 1948, and at the Warsaw Uprising Museum.

did **you** know?

...it's here?

71

Athens

WITH A POPULATION OF NEARLY 11 MILLION, ATHENS IS A BUSY PLACE BY DAY AND NIGHT, BUT ITS CITIZENS RETAIN AN ENVIABLY RELAXED ATTITUDE TO LIFE.

antiquity &
presence

- Athens' most potent symbol is the Acropolis hill, topped by the dramatic remains of the Parthenon, a Doric temple dating from 477BC.

- The temple was dedicated to the goddess Athena, from whom the city takes its name.

evocative &
majestic

- Historic remains litter the city, and include the Roman Agora and the Tower of the Winds— a tower dating to the first century BC that functioned as a sundial and a weather vane.

- Fifteen majestic, weathered stone columns (of an original 104) still stand at the Temple of Olympian Zeus, which was built in the second century AD.

Q *When was the first modern Olympic Games held?* **A** *In 1896, here in Athens.*

Ελλάδα

economy &
evolution

- Much of the city's original wealth was founded on shipping, and was linked to the vast nearby trading port of Pireaus.

- Today its industries are slowly declining, but the entry of Greece into the European Union in 1981 gave it an economic boost, and in 1985 Athens became the first declared Cultural Capital of Europe.

- Tourism and service industries have a major part to play in the city's continued success.

did **you** know?

...it's here?

spectacle &
drama

- Athens pulled out all the stops to prepare the city's infrastructure for the Olympic Games of 2004, judged a huge success.

- More than 10,000 athletes took part in the games, and fabulous firework displays lit up the city for the spectacle of the opening and closing ceremonies.

At midday in Athens it is 6am in Santo Domingo and 11am in Prague...   *...do you know where they are?*

Istanbul

ISTANBUL, THE LARGEST CITY IN TURKEY, STRADDLES THE CONTINENTS OF EUROPE AND
ASIA, AND KEEPS ONE FOOT FIRMLY IN EACH CULTURE.

vital &
commercial

- Istanbul is a vital trading port on the
  Bosphorous Strait, a narrow channel that
  links the Sea of Marmara to the Black Sea.
  A busy stream of tankers and container ships
  occupies it every minute of the day.

- The city has a population of 11 million, who pay
  half of the income tax in the whole country.

- Ancient and modern meet here, with fine old
  churches and mosques, and dusty backstreets
  where women cover their heads around one
  corner, and trendy cafés and people in the
  latest Western fashions around the next.

- Its rich multicultural mix means that the city
  has built up a cultural life to rival the best
  in Europe, with events including a major
  international arts festival.

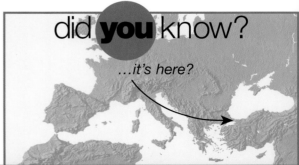

did **you** know?

...it's here?

Türkiye

historic &
religious

- The city was named Constantinople after the Roman Emperor Constantine the Great, who introduced Christianity to the region.

- It became capital of the eastern Roman Empire, then, in 1453, the capital of the Ottoman Empire. It was renamed Istanbul in 1930.

- Its most famous historic sites include the Imperial Sultanahmet Mosque (Blue Mosque), and the Topkapi Palace (home to one of the biggest diamonds in the world, known as the Spoonmaker's).

At midday in Istanbul it is 11am in Stockholm and 5pm in Hanoi...   *...do you know where they are?*

Jerusalem

ישראל ירושלים

Israel

JERUSALEM IS AN ANCIENT CITY RESONANT WITH RELIGIOUS
HISTORY FOR MUSLIMS, CHRISTIANS, AND JEWS ALIKE.

Q What does the arch in this photograph represent?

A The ruins of the Hurva Synagogue, in the Jewish Quarter.

At midday in Jerusalem it is 11am in Geneva and 3am in Denver...   *...do you know where they are?*

TIME ZONE: JERUSALEM GMT+2

political &
religious

- Fought over for centuries by different religious groups with rival claims, Jerusalem has an Old Town that is divided into Armenian, Christian, Jewish, and Muslim quarters.

- The first to claim victory was King David in 1005BC. King Solomon built the first Jewish Temple there, but in AD70 the city was all but wiped out by the Romans.

- Over the next 600 years it passed through Christian Byzantine hands, then to the Arabs, before eventually passing to the Ottoman Turks in 1517.

- In 1948 Israel took over the west of the city from Palestine, and in 1967 annexed the eastern sector as well.

- The Church of the Holy Sepulchre, built on the spot where Christ was crucified, buried, and resurrected, is shared by six Christian denominations. To prevent arguments between the factions, the keys have been entrusted to a Muslim family since 1187.

ancient &
gilded

- The blue-tiled, golden-domed Muslim temple known as the Dome of the Rock, is the best known structure in the city, rising above the surrounding historic buildings on Temple Mount.

- The Al-Aqsa Mosque, also located on Temple Mount, is the oldest in the world, and dates back to AD715.

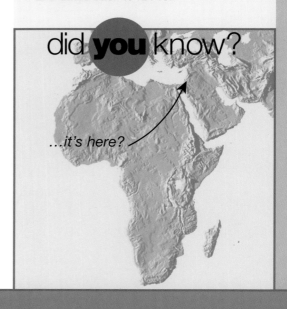

did **you** know?

...it's here?

Cairo

EGYPT'S CAPITAL IS ONE OF THE MOST ANCIENT CITIES IN THE WORLD, YET BOASTS A MODERN METRO SYSTEM, OPENED AS RECENTLY AS 1987.

divided &
prosperous

● Cairo was founded in AD969 (more than 3,000 years after the building of the Great Pyramid at nearby Giza) at the point where the River Nile divides into three branches.

● Today, with a population of over 15 million, it is Africa's biggest city.

● The oldest part, Fustat, lies east of the river, and is characterized by narrow lanes and haphazard, crowded tenements. The modern city is on the west bank and was laid out in the 19th century to echo the open style of Paris.

● Much of the country's greatest art is held in the Egyptian Museum, including the treasures of Tutankhamun's tomb.

did **you** know?

...it's here?

At midday in Cairo it is 5am in Bogotá and 10am in Edinburgh...   *...do you know where they are?*

Johannesburg

JOHANNESBURG TURNED A MAJOR CORNER WHEN APARTHEID POLICIES WERE FINALLY BANNED IN 1991, AND IT IS NOW A BUSY MODERN CITY.

Q Can you guess how many trees are planted around the city?

A More than 10 million.

TIME ZONE: JOHANNESBURG GMT+2

South Africa

boomtown &
modernity

- Johannesburg is a city founded on gold. Until 1866 it was little more than high grassland, but the coming of the prospectors soon made it the biggest settlement in South Africa.

- It is estimated that 40 percent of the world's gold has been mined around Johannesburg.

- By 1875 its population stood at around 100,000, most of whom worked in the mines. Today the population is around 3.2 million.

- Modern Johannesburg is an energetic, sprawling metropolis, comparable in size to Los Angeles.

- The legacy of racial segregation and Apartheid policies is still widely seen across the city, with comparably high rates of poverty and unemployment among the masses, while the rich barricade themselves behind high walls and rely on intruder alarms and armed response units for their security.

- The Apartheid Museum evokes the struggles of those living in the city's segregated townships in the 1970s and '80s, showing the worst while exposing the futility of Apartheid policies, and demonstrating how Johannesburg and the South African nation have survived them.

did **you** know?

...it's here?

At midday in Johannesburg it is 4am in Winnipeg and 6pm in Kuala Lumpur...   *...do you know where they are?*

Cape Town

DOMINATED BY THE UNMISTAKABLE FLATTENED PEAK OF TABLE MOUNTAIN, CAPE TOWN IS SOUTH AFRICA'S DRAMATICALLY SET GARDEN CITY.

Q *When was the Cape first settled?* **A** *Around 100,000 years ago.*

South Africa

diversity &
vitality

- Ruled at different times by the Portuguese and the British, Cape Town has a rich ethnic and cultural mix. Wealthy, attractive suburbs contrast with the impoverished Cape Flats townships, where most Capetonians live.

- Despite the social divide, each of Cape Town's unique suburbs has a rare vitality about it, with beach volleyball, gleaming skyscrapers, and craft markets all part of the blend.

- The city's Victoria and Albert Waterfront is the most popular tourist attraction in the country.

remarkable &
uplifting

- Offshore Robben Island is notorious for its prison, where the black rights campaigner Nelson Mandela was imprisoned for 21 years from 1963.

- Mandela wrote movingly of his time on Robben Island in his autobiography, *The Long Road to Freedom*.

- Today the prison is a museum, and former political prisoners act as guides, demonstrating to the world how even the worst hardships can be overcome.

did **you** know?

...it's here?

At midday in Cape Town it is 8pm in Vladivostok and 11am in Madrid...

...do you know where they are?

St. Petersburg

THIS GRAND AND BEAUTIFUL NEO-CLASSICAL CITY IS WIDELY REGARDED AS THE MOST
PROGRESSIVE, LIBERAL, AND WESTERNIZED IN RUSSIA.

Q *After which Soviet hero was the city renamed in the 20th century?*

A *Vladimir Ilyich Lenin (1870–1924).*

TIME ZONE: ST. PETERSBURG GMT+3

Россия

classical & **elegant**

- Peter the Great was determined to have a new city that could build him a navy and be his "Window on the West." Started in 1703, it was built on a marsh around the River Niva.

- Between 1712 and 1918 it was the capital of Russia, and many of the elegant neo-classical palaces, churches, and tree-lined squares date from the prosperous reign of Catherine the Great (1729–96).

- The city resonates with past grandeur, from the House of Fabergé to the Hermitage, one of the most celebrated art museums in the world.

- St. Petersburg has always been a magnet for artists, and past residents include the writers Pushkin, Gogol, and Dostoyevsky, and composers Rimsky-Korsakov and Borodin.

history & **politics**

- St. Petersburg is home to the most famous ballet company in the world: the Kirov. The company has its own theater, and the Imperial Ballet School.

- Kirov dancers reintroduced classical ballet to Western Europe in the early 20th century, producing stars such as Anna Pavlova and Mikhail Barishnikov.

did **you** know?

...*it's here?*

Moscow

THE RUSSIAN CAPITAL HAS SHED MUCH OF ITS IMAGE OF COMMUNIST GLOOM, TO BECOME A MORE COSMOPOLITAN AND FASHION-CONSCIOUS CITY.

architecture & politics

- The imposing Kremlin fortress lines one side of the Moskva River, its golden domes and gothic spires peeping over the walls and around the palaces of the former Soviet powerhouse.

- The skyline has been joined recently by the new symbols of capitalism: glass and steel tower blocks.

- The city's new shopping malls and businesses reflect the boom in consumer spending.

unexpected & unusual

- The colorful minarets of St. Basil's Cathedral look Disneyesque in daylight, but theatrically dramatic when floodlit by night.

- Moscow's underground rail system is unique, with many of the stations fabulously decorated and more like palaces than transport hubs. Check out the marble halls and chandeliers of the Komsomolskya station.

- The enormous GUM department store on Red Square is stuffed full of chic designer shops— it's all a far cry from Communist days, when there was often little to buy here.

Россия

Q *Where is the world's largest bell (200 tonnes)?*

A *Within the Kremlin—but it cracked in the foundry and has never been rung.*

? The modern monument known as the Space Obelisk reminds Moscovites of their continuing role in the space race.

did **you** know?

...it's here?

At midday in Moscow it is 4am in Lima and 5pm in Hong Kong...　　　　　*...do you know where they are?*

Dubai

DUBAI HAS EMERGED IN RECENT YEARS AS A LUXURY PLAYGROUND FOR THE RICH AND FAMOUS, AND A SHOPPING PARADISE, ESPECIALLY FOR THOSE SEEKING GOLD.

sunshine &
oil barrels

- Nomads were calling into Dubai Creek from the third century BC, but it's only since the 19th century that a small settlement grew up here.

- Everything changed with the discovery of oil in 1966, enabling the rapid generation of incredible wealth.

- As Dubai earned billions of dollars from oil, it invested in the country's infrastructure and conjured up a city to match its new-found riches.

- Now petroleum products account for only around 10 percent of Dubai's economy, and sunshine and sandy shores are taking over as the city's chief asset, drawing thousands of tourists each year.

 Q *What is the main attraction at the new Dubailand theme park?*

 A *A ski center—with real snow!*

development &
growth

- Around 60 percent of the city's 1 million population is made up of immigrant workers from India, Pakistan, and the Philippines. They make up a workforce that is a vital part of the city's rapid growth.

- New building projects have been on a grand scale, reflecting imagination and innovation as well as luxury and excess.

- Dubai's most remarkable building to date is the Burj al Arab luxury hotel, a sail-shaped structure on its own purpose-built island that has come to symbolize the new face of the city.

- Among extraordinary new building projects is the hotel made up of some 300 little man-made islands, reclaimed from the waters of the Arabian Gulf, and shaped into a map of the world, that opened in 2005.

did **you** know?

...it's here?

Delhi

GRACIOUS, ORDERED NEW DELHI CONTRASTS WITH THE HISTORIC RICHES AND CHAOTIC LIFE OF OLD DELHI IN INDIA'S GREAT CAPITAL CITY.

historic &
central

- Delhi grew up in the 17th century as the capital of the Moghul Empire.

- Its most influential builder of the time was Shah Jahan (1592–1666), whose architectural legacy includes the exquisite Taj Mahal, the imposing Red Fort and the vast Jama Masjid, or Friday Mosque, which can hold up to 25,000 worshipers in its courtyard alone.

- When the British took control of India they moved the capital to Calcutta, but it reverted in 1911 with a massive project to build an imperial New Delhi of wide, tree-lined avenues and imposing government buildings.

- A population of almost 19 million people and 3.3 million vehicles means the city has a perennial traffic problem—which it aims to resolve by building a brand new metro system.

did **you** know?

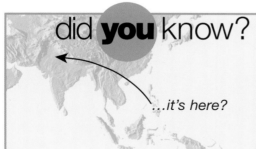

...it's here?

Bhārata Gaṇarājya

Q *Which well-known English architect designed New Delhi?*

A *Sir Edwin Lutyens (1869–1944).*

At midday in Delhi it is 11.30am in Tashkent and 7.30am in Manchester…   *…do you know where they are?*

Kolkata

Kolkata, renamed from Calcutta in 2001, is one of India's pre-eminent economic hubs, and has the biggest cricket stadium in the world.

did **you** know?

...it's here?

Q What is the name of the taxi carriages pulled by men in the city?

A Rickshaws.

🌐 *TIME ZONE: KOLKATA GMT+5.5*

Bhārata Gaṇarājya

imperial &
industrial

- Kolkata was established as a British trading post on the Hooghly River, a tributary of the mighty Ganges, by the Bay of Bengal, in 1690.

- From 1772 to 1911 it served as the capital of British India, and today Kolkata is still the capital of West Bengal.

- The elaborate Victoria Memorial is just one legacy of its imperial past—a grandiose, white-domed building started in 1906, which now serves as a museum to the British Raj and is the city's art gallery.

- A major port, Kolkata's economy is rooted in industrial, trade, and financial activities, with electronics, printing, publishing, and newspaper production also playing an important role.

heroes &
heroines

- Rabindranath Tagore (1861–1941), born in Kolkata, was awarded the Nobel Prize for Literature in 1913.

- Tagore was a poet and novelist, penning the words for India's national anthem, and devoting much of his life to promoting educational reform across the region of Bengal.

- Mother Teresa (1910–97) was a remarkable woman: a Roman Catholic nun who devoted her life to the destitute people of the city, where she opened her House for the Dying in 1952. She later established a leper colony in West Bengal, and was awarded the Nobel Peace Prize in 1979.

At midday in Kolkata it is 8.30am in Zagreb and 2.30am in Kingston...　　　　　*...do you know where they are?*

Bangkok

ราชอาณาจักรไทย *Thailand*

THE THAI CAPITAL IS ONE OF THE GREAT CITIES OF ASIA,
CRISS-CROSSED BY ELEVATED SUPER-HIGHWAYS AND STUDDED
WITH HIGH-RISE TOWERS.

Q Which Thai king featured in the popular 1951 musical, The King and I?

A King Mongkut (Rama IV), a progressive monarch and keen scientist.

At midday in Bangkok it is 2am in Buenos Aires and 6am in Copenhagen…   *…do you know where they are?*

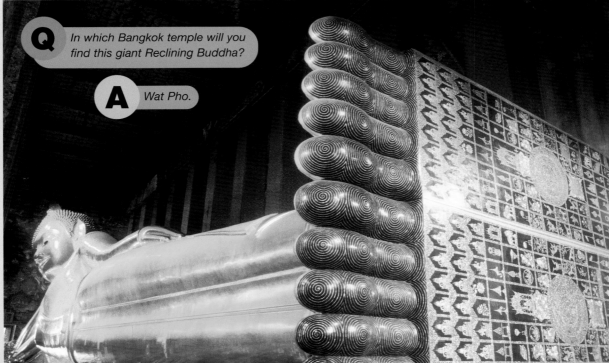

Q In which Bangkok temple will you find this giant Reclining Buddha?

A Wat Pho.

water-bound &
many-centered

- The city grew up on opposing banks of the Chao Phraya River in the 18th century. Concentric rings of canals were built as a defense, and for many years it was known as "the Venice of the East."

- Ratanakosin Island is the cultural and historical heart of the city, but Bangkok is a city of many different centers. Silom Road is another—all the major banking and trading institutions are here.

- Patpong, at one end of Silom Road, is the center of entertainment and has a vibrant night-life, including the famous night market.

- Stylish shopping malls have appeared in the city in recent years, and the shoppers' paradise is generally considered to be Sukhumvit Road.

religion &
culture

- King Rama I (1732–1809) gave the city a Thai name that is the longest in the world, comprising 164 letters. It is usually shortened by Thais to Krung Thep, meaning City of Angels.

- The city has many magnificent Buddhist temples, of which the most spectacular is Wat Phra Kaew, built in 1784.

- Wat Phra Kaew was built to house Thailand's most sacred image, the tiny Emerald Buddha. Standing just 30 inches (75cm) high, the image, carved from jasper, stands in the middle of the temple on a high pedestal, protected by glass, and surrounded by an aura of mystery and respect.

did **you** know?

...it's here?

Ho Chi Minh City

VIETNAM'S SECOND CITY HAS HAD A CHECKERED HISTORY, AND IS TODAY A BUSTLING HIVE OF INDUSTRY AND ACTIVITY.

facts & **figures**

- Ho Chi Minh City is the largest in Vietnam, with a population just under 5 million.

- Its ethnic mix is 80 percent Vietnamese and 20 percent Chinese, whose traditional Chinatown enclave is known by the old name of Cholon.

- The major port for the fertile Mekong Delta and southern Vietnam, its main exports are agricultural produce (notably rice), rubber, coal, minerals, crude petroleum, ores, and seafood.

history & **change**

- Until the 17th century this was little more than a small Khmer fishing settlement, called Prey Nokor—a name still widely used by Cambodian nationalists today.

- Renamed Saigon by the Vietnamese, it was seized by France in 1859 and became the capital of the French colony of Cochinchina.

- From 1956 Saigon was the capital of the US-backed Republic of Vietnam, but after the Communists took over in 1975 the power passed to Hanoi, and the city was renamed.

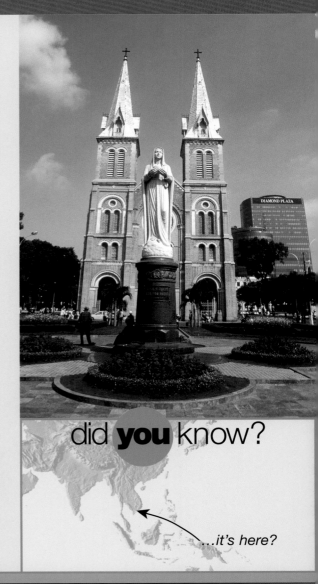

did **you** know?

...it's here?

Việt Nam

modernizer &
leader

- The city is named for the man regarded as the father of modern Vietnam, Nguyen Sinh Cung (1890–1969), who took the name Ho Chi Minh ("he who Enlightens") in 1930.

- A committed Communist, he sought independence from French rule for Vietnam after 1941, finally achieving this in 1952. He died in 1969, six years before his dream of the reunification of North and South Vietnam was realized.

Ho Chi Minh City *Vietnam*

 Q *What is the name given to the conical straw hats worn by some Vietnamese?*

 A Non la.

Kuala Lumpur

Post-colonial Kuala Lumpur (or "KL" as it is sometimes known) is the largest city in Malaysia, and the booming capital of the Federation.

Q Which building overtook the Petronas Twin Towers in the record books in 2003?

A Taiwan's Taipei 101.

Persekutuan Malaysia

record-breaking & **superlative**

- The Petronas Twin Towers, completed in 1998, were designed to be the tallest structures in the world. Eighty-eight floors loom above the popular Suria KLCC shopping center, the towers linked by a "sky bridge."

- Kuala Lumpur also claims the world's highest flagpole, 328 feet (100m) high.

? Kuala Lumpur's population is a cosmopolitan mixture of Malays (58 percent), Chinese (31 percent), Indians (8 percent), and other nationalities (3 percent).

post-colonial & **modernizing**

- Kuala Lumpur grew up around a rough Chinese tin-mining settlement in the mid-19th century, later developing an attractive colonial style of architecture that combined European, Chinese, and Moorish traditions—the railway station is the epitome of this.

- The city was occupied by Japanese forces in World War II, and gained independence from Britain in 1957.

- The Asian economic boom of the 1990s brought new wealth and confidence to Kuala Lumpur, a boost that is reflected in its new skyscraper skyline and architectural styling.

- Today the city is trying to bring the transport infrastructure up to speed with the rest of its rapid growth, introducing a Rapid Transit rail system in 1992, and a high-speed rail link to the international airport in 2002.

did **you** know?

...it's here?

103

Singapore

A TINY INDEPENDENT REPUBLIC, SINGAPORE IS A SLEEK MODERN CITY WITH A TEEMING MULTILAYERED CULTURE JUST BENEATH THE SURFACE.

ultramodern &
high-rise

- Singapore is a bustling business capital, the second-richest country in Asia, dominated by the steel and glass towers of high finance.

- Despite a somewhat sterile appearance, Singapore's rich diversity is reflected in its distinctive ethnic enclaves, with Chinese, Indian, Malaysian, Arab, and European quarters to discover.

? Singapore has the second highest population density in the world: 16,786 people per square mile (6,481 per sq km).

Q *Where do the locals hang out at weekends?*

A *Sentosa Island, a pleasure park with an imported sandy beach, museums, aquariums, and sports facilities.*

 TIME ZONE: SINGAPORE GMT+8

Republik Singapura

proud &
colonial

- Modern Singapore was founded as a British colonial trading post by Sir Thomas Stamford Raffles in 1819.

- The magnificent old Raffles Hotel is still the place to sip a refreshing pink "Singapore Sling" cocktail, while following the tradition of dropping your pistachio-nut shells on the floor of the bar.

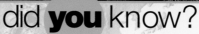

did **you** know?

...it's here?

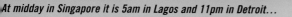

Hong Kong

? The world's steepest railway runs to the viewpoint at the top of Victoria Peak—carriages take eight minutes to reach the top.

did **you** know?

...it's here?

TIME ZONE: HONG KONG GMT+8

history &
geography

- Hong Kong was founded by Britain on a barren rock in 1841, and a 99-year lease on the territories was formally taken out in 1898.

- In 1997 Hong Kong reverted to Chinese rule, although it will retain a high degree of autonomy until 2047. Its population makes it the fourth-largest city in China.

- The city is divided into four main areas: Kowloon, the New Territories, Hong Kong Island, and the Outlying Islands. The first two are on a peninsula attached to the Chinese mainland, Hong Kong Island is on the southern side of the harbor facing Kowloon, and there are 234 Outlying Islands.

- Most of the 7.3 million people in Hong Kong live in high-rise apartment blocks around the city. Beyond the city limits, 60 percent of the land is protected parkland.

Q *Which is the predominant form of religion in Hong Kong?*

A Ancestor Worship.

At midday in Hong Kong it is 6am in Tallinn and 10am in Novosibirsk...

...do you know where they are?

107

Shanghai

CHINA'S BOOMING, ULTRAMODERN CITY IS IN A STRATEGIC TRADING POSITION AT THE MOUTH OF THE YANGTZE RIVER.

tea houses & **modern towers**

- The Oriental Pearl Tower, opened in 1993 and the symbol of the ultramodern city. Don't miss the Jin Mao Tower, the fourth-highest building in the world at 1,381ft (421m).

- "Old Shanghai", the downtown area once encircled by city walls, is being restored and rebuilt. It centers around the famous Huxingting Tea House and the tranquil Yu Yuan Garden.

- Fangbang Zhonglu, in the old town, is a restored street lined with traditional Shanghai dumpling houses, bric-a-brac stores, and art galleries. Here, red Chinese lanterns cast their atmospheric glow over reproduction 1930s posters and Chairman Mao memorabilia.

history & **population**

- Shanghai was promoted from a fishing village to a commercial town in 1074.

- The Japanese, latest in a long line of occupiers, moved out in 1945, sparking a rush to rebuild and reinvigorate the city.

- It is the birthplace of "the Mother of China", Soong Ching-ling (1893–1981), outspoken wife of the Chinese Republic's founder, Sun Yat-sen.

- The population of the city is now 20,000,000 and is increasing rapidly.

- Shanghai is the home of the world's fastest Maglev (magnetic levitation) train, which can reach speeds of up to 188mph (300kph).

did **you** know?

...it's here?

TIME ZONE: SHANGHAI GMT+8

中华人民共和国

Q *Which part of Shanghai is this?*

景容楼

老廟黄金

'97上海旅游节黄金首饰珠宝博览会
老庙黄金足金豪华套装展销

A *It is part of the main shopping area in the largely rebuilt Old Town (Nanshi) of Shanghai.*

At midday in Shanghai it is 11pm in Philadelphia and 5am in Dubrovnik...   *...do you know where they are?*

Beijing

CHINA'S CAPITAL AND SECOND-LARGEST CITY IS ONE OF THE GREAT CITIES OF THE WORLD, WITH A HISTORY AND CULTURE THAT TRULY DAZZLES.

did **you** know?

....it's here?

TIME ZONE: BEIJING GMT+8

People's Republic of China

中华人民共和国

Q *Which world sporting event will take place here in 2008?*

A *The Olympic Games.*

landmarks & **history**

● Tiananmen Square is the largest public square in the world. The Mao mausoleum at its southern end contains the embalmed body of Mao Zedong (1893–1976), the Communist hero who overthrew the imperial powers in 1949.

● Museums on the eastern side of the square record Beijing's history, from its start in AD700 as a tiny trading post, to the Opium Wars of the 19th century and the Revolution of the 20th century.

● Other historical landmarks include the wooden Drum Tower, the Bell Tower, and the superb Temple of Heaven.

secret & **impressive**

● The Forbidden City is the name given to Beijing's Imperial Palace. With 9,999 rooms, it is the biggest palace complex in the world, and has been rebuilt many times—but always to the original design.

● The Forbidden City was established between 1406 and 1420 by the Ming emperor Yongle (Chengzu), and was home to China's emperors until 1911.

Perth

THE LURES OF SUN, SEA, AND ALFRESCO LIVING DRAW MORE THAN 3 MILLION TOURISTS EACH YEAR TO THIS POPULAR WESTERN AUSTRALIAN CITY.

sunshine &
location

- Perth owes its popularity to its sunshine record (even the winter temperatures average out at 64°F/18°C) and its idyllic location on the Swan River, where it spills out into the Indian Ocean.

- The natural resources of gold and minerals made this a wealthy city in the late 19th century, and the standard of living today is comfortably high.

- In 1970 the Indian Pacific Railway was finally completed, making a direct link to Sydney and ending almost a century of isolation from southeastern Australia.

- Fremantle, the port just south of Perth, became known as the Gateway to Australia, as convicts gave way to free settlers and then tourists. Its historic sites include Australia's oldest public building, the Round House.

Q What is the name of Perth's major wine-growing area?

A The Swan Valley Wine Region.

did **you** know?

...it's here?

At midday in Perth it is 10pm in Guatemala and 5am in Brussels...

...do you know where they are?

Tokyo

Tokyo is a powerhouse of creative energy, global influence, and wealth, a 24-hour city still remarkably free of crime.

Q What is the name of Tokyo's high-speed train service?

A The Shinkansen.

did **you** know?

...it's here?

TIME ZONE: TOKYO GMT+9

日本国

extremes &
superlatives

- A staggering one quarter of the entire population of Japan lives within a 30-mile (48km) radius of Tokyo's Imperial Palace.

- The Imperial Palace at the heart of Tokyo, dating back to 1868, is said to be the world's most valuable piece of real estate.

- Tsujiki, Tokyo's wholesale seafood market, is the biggest fish market in the world.

- Eating out is an essential part of daily life in Tokyo, and as a result the city has a fabulous variety of restaurants.

- Just 15 minutes away from downtown by train, Tokyo Disneyland is said to be the world's most visited theme park.

history &
culture

- Few of Tokyo's older buildings survived the American fire bombing of World War II, but tradition lives on in the modern city in such things as social values and etiquette.

- The city includes the highly industrialized area of Kanto, with the ports of Kawasaki and Yokohama.

- The city is a fashionista's dream. The stores of local fashion superstars Issey Miyake and Yohji Yamamoto are both in the Aoyama district.

- Peace can be found at the tranquil and beautiful Meiji Shrine, a train ride away from busy downtown at Harajuku.

Sydney
Australia

CLEAR AIR, SUNSHINE, TOP-CLASS RESTAURANTS, AND A VIBRANT CULTURE AND NIGHTLIFE ARE JUST SOME OF THE ELEMENTS THAT MAKE SYDNEY SO POPULAR.

Q   What is the local nickname for Sydney's Harbour Bridge?

A   The Coathanger.

At midday in Sydney it is 2am in Dublin and 10am in Singapore…   *…do you know where they are?*

history &
growth

- Long before the first explorers and convict ships arrived from Europe, the area around Sydney was known to local tribes as Warren.

- By 1790 the British penal colony here numbered about 10,000.

- The Harbour Bridge—the world's largest single-span steel arch bridge—was built in 1932.

- The city's second iconic landmark is the remarkable Opera House, dating from 1973.

- The year 2000 marked a new confidence in Sydney's populace, when the city hosted the Olympic Games. The Games were widely acclaimed as the best in modern times, boosting tourism and the economy.

- A society where myriad cultures co-exist in harmony is the basis of Sydney's "no worries" mentality—the catch-phrase of a liberal people intent on enjoying each day as it comes.

relaxation &
beach life

- Australians worship the beach, and Sunday afternoon excursions are a national institution, and there's plenty of choice around Sydney.

- More than 50,000 sun-worshipers and surfers have been known to congregate on the famous Bondi Beach on a summer's day.

- The name Bondi comes from an Aboriginal word that translates as "the sound of waves breaking on a beach."

- The suburb of Manly is another seaside playground, where a white-sand beach is backed by towering Norfolk pines. Numerous outdoor cafés add to the excitement.

- Darling Harbor, in the shadow of the downtown skyscrapers, is a leisure oasis of a different kind, offering local people and visitors street entertainment, Chinese gardens, a casino, an IMAX movie theater and an aquarium, with a monorail to link them all together.

did **you** know?

...it's here?

Melbourne

PERHAPS LACKING THE SAME YOUTHFUL DRIVE AS SYDNEY AND PERTH, MELBOURNE IS A GENTLER, CALMER CITY WITH A LIFE OF ITS OWN.

history &
technology

- Modern Melbourne is a product of the gold rush of 1851, which brought thousands of prospectors to this coastal capital of the newly founded state of Victoria.

- The extravagant 19th-century buildings that take center-stage on Melbourne's grid-like streets and recount its history are a reminder of its past and present prosperity.

- Today the city's economy is flourishing, with a focus on new technologies.

 Melbourne has the third largest tram network in the world, and more than 100 million tram rides are taken every year.

did **you** know?

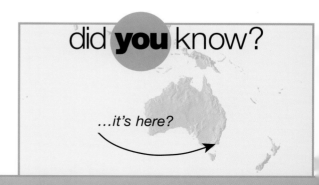

...it's here?

TIME ZONE: MELBOURNE GMT+10

 Q Where in Melbourne can you find a small colony of wild penguins?

 A On the shore at St. Kilda.

sporty &
passionate

- The Commonwealth Games in 2006 proved the perfect excuse to upgrade sporting facilities around the city.

- The Australian Rules Football Grand Final, the prestigious Australian Tennis Open, and a Formula One Grand Prix are just some of the other major sporting events held here.

- Entertainment can be found at the Luna Park pleasure complex along the coast at St. Kilda, a suburb with one of the city's top beaches.

At midday in Melbourne it is 2am in Marrakech and 10am in Shanghai…   *…do you know where they are?*

Auckland

New Zealand's largest and most prosperous city, Auckland has a reputation for its Maori culture and the quality of its sailing.

sky-high &
adrenaline-fueled

- Auckland's Sky Tower is the tallest structure in the southern hemisphere, at 1,076 feet (328m), and gives spectacular panoramas over the city.

- A steady stream of young adrenaline-junkies chooses to jump (safely) from just underneath the viewing platform. From here they launch themselves toward the busy street below.

explorer &
hero

- The Auckland-born climber Edmund Hillary became a world hero in 1953 when he became the first man to climb Mount Everest.

- "Sir Ed" is celebrated in New Zealand for his charitable work, too, notably through his Himalayan Trust, which has built schools, clinics, and hospitals in Nepal.

Q *Which anti-nuclear protest ship was sunk by the French in Auckland harbor in 1985?*

A Greenpeace's Rainbow Warrior.

New Zealand

? In 2000 Auckland's harbor received a facelift ready for its role as host of the prestigious Americas Cup sailing race.

seabound &
cultural

- Auckland is set on a narrow peninsula on New Zealand's North Island, sandwiched between two harbors.

- It is actually constructed on an area of 60 dormant volcanoes—Mount Eden and One Tree Hill are just two of the most obvious volcanic mounds.

- The city emerged in the mid-19th century, and served for a short time as the capital of New Zealand.

- Auckland is a center for Maori culture, with an outstanding collection of art and artifacts held in the Auckland Museum.

- Local Maori tribes were embroiled in their own war when the first British settlers arrived, and Maori relations with the Pakeha (white population) in the city have not always been smooth.

did **you** know?

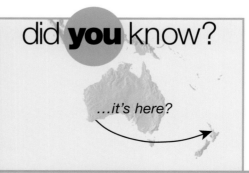

...it's here?

Vancouver

Built around a series of channels, bays, and inlets, Vancouver is a sparkling city sheltered from the full Pacific force by Vancouver Island.

sparkling &
multicultural

● With a population of fewer than 600,000, Vancouver is a melting-pot of nationalities including Indians, Japanese, and Greeks.

● It has the third-biggest Chinatown in the world, with the first classical Chinese garden ever to be built outside that country.

● Distinctive landmarks in the city include the white "sails" on the roof of the Convention Center, built as part of the World Exposition and centenary celebrations in 1986.

● Expect more innovative architecture as Vancouver prepares to host the Winter Olympics in 2010.

● Offshore Vancouver Island is easily reached by seaplane or ferry, and offers a view of quaint colonialism with its red double-decker buses and stone-built Parliament Building.

arts &
entertainment

● Vancouver has become the center of First Nation and Inuit art, with an unrivaled collection at the Museum of Anthropology.

● The city has gained the nickname "Hollywood of the North," with a TV and movie industry that brings about $1 billion each year to the region.

did **you** know?

...it's here?

Vancouver *Canada*

? Stanley Park is the city's lungs, surrounded by ocean on three sides, and the largest urban park in North America.

Q *Which international eco-protest group was founded here in 1969?*

A Greenpeace.

- At midday in Vancouver it is 10pm in Harare and 12am in Dubai...   *...do you know where they are?*

Seattle

A LIVELY, CULTURED, AND COSMOPOLITAN CITY ON AMERICA'S NORTHWEST SEABOARD, SEATTLE IS HOME TO MICROSOFT AND AMAZON.COM.

history & architecture

- The settlement of Seattle began around 1851, and the new town that built up on Elliott Bay was named after a local Indian chief.

- It soon developed into a major port, and financial and trade center, but was devastated by a massive fire in 1889. A few older buildings along the waterfront survive from this time, but most were destroyed.

- During World War II fortunes revived as local firm Boeing made military airplanes, growing by the 1960s to be the world's leading producer of commercial jet aircraft.

- A native of Seattle, entrepreneur Bill Gates founded his multi-million dollar software Microsoft technology empire in the city (along with childhood friend Paul Allen) in 1975.

- Microsoft, which has its headquarters in the suburb of Redwood, is now one of the major employers in the city, and has brought new wealth and energy to Seattle.

- You can't go far in Seattle without a coffee fix—Starbucks opened its first coffee shop in Pike Place Market in 1971.

Seattle *USA*

highlights *&* **markets**

- Seattle's most famous landmark, now almost dwarfed by the skyscrapers of downtown, is the Space Needle, a futuristic viewing tower built as a highlight of the World's Fair in 1962.

- The Needle is the focal point of the Seattle Center, a vibrant modern arts complex which is home to the prestigious Seattle Opera and Pacific Northwest Ballet.

- The harbors around the city are full of leisure sailing craft, and regular ferries serve the outlying islands and peninsulas.

- Pike Place Market, on the waterfront, is the oldest continually operating farmers' market in the US and dates back to 1907.

- The market is best known for the fantastic variety and quality of its fresh fish and seafood, but separate sections sell wonderful fresh fruit, vegetables, and flowers from across Washington State, too.

did **you** know?

...it's here?

San Francisco

FOUNDED BY FRANCISCAN FRIARS IN THE 18TH CENTURY, SAN FRANCISCO IS ONE OF THE BEST-LOVED CITIES ON THE WESTERN SEABOARD.

? The city was at the center of the dot-com boom which peaked in 2001, with computer giants Apple and Yahoo setting up in "Silicon Valley" just to the south.

San Francisco *USA*

multi-level &
multi-cultural

- San Francisco, spread over 43 hills, is known for precipitous streets, and for its historic cable cars, which run with a top speed of just 9mph (14.5kph).

- San Francisco Bay accommodates 14 islands, including the island of the notorious former state penitentiary, Alcatraz.

- The city's best-loved landmark is the Golden Gate Bridge, a red-painted suspension bridge constructed in 1937 that carries around 41 million vehicles each year.

- The laid-back reputation of its citizens dates back to the hippy revolution of the 1960s, a youthful cultural revolution which started here, introducing the world to free love and "flower power" (or peace).

- It's still a bohemian city, known for its integrated gay community. The city has a diverse population with many Hispanics, Asians (particularly Chinese), and African Americans, as well as natives of Hawaii and Alaska.

Q *When was San Francisco's last major earthquake?*

A *In 1989.*

did **you** know?

...it's here?

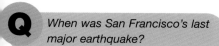

At midday in San Francisco it is 2am in Dhaka and 11pm in Antanarivo...   ...do you know where they are?

129

Los Angeles

THE "CITY OF ANGELS" IS A VAST IMAGE-CONSCIOUS METROPOLIS, AND THE SPIRITUAL HOME OF THE GREAT AMERICAN MOVIE INDUSTRY.

Q How high are the letters on the Hollywood sign?

A They stand 50 feet (15m) high.

celebrity &
urban sprawl

- On average, 50 productions a day are being filmed on these streets, just part of a Californian motion picture industry worth an annual $31 billion.

- LA has a reputation for glamour—a home to movie star legends who leave their handprints on the sidewalk outside Mann's Chinese Theater.

- The highlight of the city's celebrity year is "Oscars" night, when the great and good of the film industry honor their own, and the emotional tears and red-carpet fashions are all part of the fun.

- The Hollywood sign on Mount Lee was first erected in 1923 to advertise real estate, and is now a designated Cultural Historical Monument.

- The city is hemmed into the coast by mountains, which causes some pollution problems, and sprawls for 81 miles (130km) up the California shore.

- As the main point of entry for immigrants to the USA, Los Angeles embraces a wide variety of nationalities, including Mexicans, Armenians, and Filipinos. The city's population is almost 4 million.

? The most famous mouse in the world, Mickey Mouse, was created here by cartoonist Walt Disney in 1928.

did **you** know?

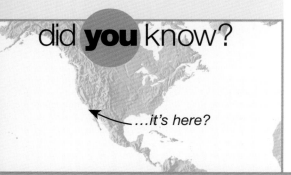

...it's here?

At midday in Los Angeles it is 2pm in Houston and 8pm in Reykjavík...   *...do you know where they are?*

Las Vegas

A BRASH, BRIGHTLY LIT PLAYGROUND FOR ADULTS AND FAMILIES ALIKE, LAS VEGAS HAS BEEN DUBBED THE ENTERTAINMENT CAPITAL OF THE WORLD.

luxury &
entertainment

- You can't miss the famous "Strip", an avenue 4.5 miles (7km) long, cruised by stretch limousines and lined with eccentric and extravagant hotels which have become tourist attractions in their own right.

- Some of the best hotels to see include the Egyptian-theme Luxor, shaped like a pyramid, the Bellagio with its floodlit dancing fountains, and the Venetian, complete with singing gondoliers and doubling as the Guggenheim Hermitage Museum.

- Look out for a wedding party. Around 150 ceremonies take place in the city every day, many in the 40 or so wedding chapels, but also in hotels and hot-air balloons.

- Las Vegas is popular as a wedding venue not just for its fun—you can be married by an Elvis Presley lookalike if you choose—but also because it is easy and comparatively quick.

? Tourism, which is based around the Strip's casino hotels, brings in $32 billion a year.

did **you** know?

...it's here?

weddings & **worship**

- The town, an oasis for travelers, was first settled by Mormons in 1854, and thrived after gambling was legalized in 1931.

- Las Vegas has around 580 churches and places of worship—that's more than any other city in the United States.

- Every year around 50,000 couples choose to marry in the city.

- The population of Las Vegas has increased to 535,000 in recent years.

Las Vegas *USA*

Mexico City

THE MEXICAN CAPITAL, A VIBRANT LATIN AMERICAN CITY, IS A BREATHTAKING 7,347 FEET (2,239M) ABOVE SEA LEVEL.

Q What is the name given to traditional Mexican bands which perform in the city?

A Mariachis.

México

culture &
commerce

● Mexico City, which covers around 500 square miles (1,295 sq km), is one of the biggest cities in the world. With a population of 22 million it is also one of the most densely populated.

● It has one of the strongest economies in Central America, built on manufacturing, construction, services, finance, and tourism.

● The city has its origins in the Aztec culture of the 14th century, and boasts no fewer that five Aztec temples among its historic buildings.

● Some of the finest buildings in the city date from the 18th century, when it was under Spanish control and prospered from mining.

● The city has continued to recover and grow after the devastation of an earthquake of 1985, which reduced some areas to rubble.

did **you** know?

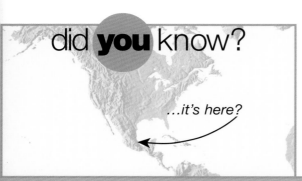

...it's here?

Chicago

CHICAGO IS THE BLUES CAPITAL OF THE WORLD, AND IS A CITY THAT LONG AGO SHED ITS PROHIBITION-ERA WILD IMAGE FOR BIG BUCKS AND BIG BUSINESS.

design & architecture

- Frank Lloyd Wright (1867–1959), the outstanding American architect of the 20th century, set up his first practise in Chicago and designed around 100 buildings in the area.

- His best-known work in the city is Robie House, which is in Hyde Park. His own former home (and studio) is now a museum, and restored to its 1909 appearance.

- According to local claims, Chicago's nine-story Home Insurance building, erected in 1885, was the world's first skyscraper.

- Other highlights include the Sears Tower (once the tallest in the world), the Wrigley Building with its clock-tower, the neo-Gothic Tribune Tower, and Frank Gehry's Music Pavilion.

Q *Which gangster and bootlegger made his name in Chicago in the "Roaring Twenties"?*

 A *Al Capone (1899–1947).*

Chicago *USA*

pleasure &
industry

● The "Windy City" is the third largest in the US, and includes 29 miles (47km) of lakefront parks and 15 miles (24km) of sparkling sandy beaches.

● Many household-name American companies have their headquarters in Chicago, including United Airlines, McDonald's, and Motorola.

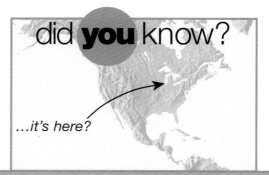

did **you** know?

...it's here?

At midday in Chicago it is 9pm in Nairobi and 7pm in Frankfurt...   *...do you know where they are?*

Québec

historic & **fortified**

- Québec has a unique status as the only fortified city in North America.

- Fortifications include the magnificent Citadelle—a star-shape fortress beside the water, built by the British to a classic French design in 1820, and still used as a military headquarters today.

- The most famous building in the city, with the appearance of a Gothic castle, is the grand Château Frontenac Hotel, built in 1893 at the height of the railway age. It has 618 rooms.

- Québec city is divided into the upper area, within the historic walls, called Vieux-Québec; and the Lower Town, built along the banks of the St. Lawrence River. The center is a square, the elegant Place Royale.

? The nearby Plains of Abraham were the site of a famous battle in 1759, when the British seized Québec from the French.

did **you** know?

...it's here?

Canada

French &
proud of it

● Ninety-five percent of the people in Québec speak French as their first language, and the city is the bastion of French culture and tradition in Canada.

● Lest they forget their origins, the Québécois carry the French phrase "*Je me souviens*" (I remember) on every car license plate.

At midday in Québec it is 7am in Honolulu and 7pm in Athens…   *…do you know where they are?*

Montréal

MONTRÉAL COPES WITH HOT SUMMER DAYS AND BITTERLY COLD WINTERS, VIA THE UNIQUE 20-MILE (32KM) UNDERGROUND VILLE SOUTERRAINE NETWORK OF WALKWAYS.

Q In which year did Montréal become the capital of a united Canada?

A In 1844.

did **you** know?

...it's here?

Canada

foundation &
growth

- Montréal was founded in 1642 as the colony of Ville-Marie, by Frenchman Paul de Chomedy.

- The fur trade eventually gave way to Montréal's development in the 19th century as a major grain port and center of manufacturing.

- The 1967 World's Fair put the city firmly on the world map, and some of its most remarkable structures, including the futuristic box-like housing on Ile St. Helene, date from this period.

- The 1976 Olympics brought the building of a metro system, the landmark Biodôme stadium (now an excellent science museum), and the extraordinary leaning panoramic viewing tower at Olympic Park.

festivals &
fun

- There are lots of festivals in this city, but two of the best known are the Just for Laughs (comedy, of course), and the International Jazz Festival.

- Ice hockey is a passion in Montréal, and the city's Canadiens Hockey Club has won the Stanley Cup a record 24 times.

At midday in Montréal it is 7pm in Sofia and 3am in Vladivostok…　　　*…do you know where they are?*

Toronto

CANADA'S BIGGEST CITY HAS SHED ITS DULL, PROVINCIAL IMAGE IN FAVOR OF BUSY REGENERATION AND A VIBRANT CULTURAL MIX.

commercial & cosmopolitan

- Once a fur-traders' outpost, Toronto is now Canada's premier commercial and banking center, with a population of just over 5 million.

- It's known as a lively and cosmopolitan city, with distinctive neighborhoods including Little India, Little Italy, and Little Portugal.

- Toronto has a billion-dollar movie-making industry, and hosts an annual International Film Festival—the largest in North America.

- Its greatest landmark is the CN Tower. At 1,814 feet (553m) it is the world's tallest freestanding structure. Exterior elevators take 2 million visitors a year to the viewing galleries.

Q Toronto's Skydome sports stadium is the home of which baseball team?

A *The Toronto Blue Jays.*

Canada

cultural &
sporty

- Many of Canada's top writers have lived here and used the city as a backdrop for their novels. They include Margaret Atwood, the late Robertson Davies, and Michael Ondaatje.

- Toronto's theater scene is the third largest in the English-speaking world (after London and New York), and notable summer theater festivals are held out of town at Stratford and Niagara-on-the-Lake.

- There are more than 120 ice rinks around the city, used both for leisure skating and the sport of ice hockey.

did **you** know?

...it's here?

143

At midday in Toronto it is 9pm in Abu Dhabi and 2pm in Rio de Janeiro...   *...do you know where they are?*

Boston

A CHECKERED HISTORY HAS SHAPED THIS GRAND OLD SEA PORT, FAMED FOR ITS ANTI-SLAVERY STANCE AND ITS IVY LEAGUE UNIVERSITY.

history &
education

- Boston was founded on America's eastern seaboard by Puritans from Britain in 1630.

- It grew to be a major port, building wealth in the 18th century on the back of slavery—and becoming the first place to abolish slavery.

- Despite racial diversity in the city, communities are polarized—Malcolm X was a resident of the largely African-American area of Roxbury, and the city suffered from race riots in the 1960s and the 1970s.

- Today high-tech industries have replaced manufacture and trade, and Boston's elegant old buildings, revamped waterfront, and whale-watching cruises are magnets for tourists.

- Boston boasts more than 30 universities and colleges. The most famous of these is Harvard University, founded in 1636.

- The Bonsai Garden at the Harvard Arboretum is more than 200 years old.

- **?** Boston claims to have the first ever subway system, the oldest university, the first public park, and the oldest botanical garden in America.

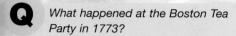

Q *What happened at the Boston Tea Party in 1773?*

A *Locals tipped 342 chests of tea into the bay in a political protest against the British.*

famous &
influential

● Benjamin Franklin, the celebrated anti-slavery pioneer who also drafted the American Declaration of Independence (1776) and invented bifocal spectacles, was born in Boston in 1706.

● Patriot Paul Revere (1734–1818) was also born here. Revere is remembered for his part in the notorious Boston Tea Party protest, and for his famous ride to Lexington and Lincoln to warn the rebels that British soldiers were on the move and heading their way.

did **you** know?

...it's here?

At midday in Boston it is 6pm in Belgrade and 3am in Singapore...

...do you know where they are?

145

New York

USA

MODERN NEW YORK WAS FOUNDED AS A DUTCH COLONY, NAMED NEW AMSTERDAM, IN 1624, AND HAS GROWN TO BECOME ONE OF THE GREAT CITIES OF THE WORLD.

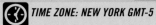

New York USA

Q Which leafy space is the city's green lung?

A Central Park.

At midday in New York it is 11am in San Salvador and 6pm in Paris…   …do you know where they are?

multi-racial &
multi-cultural

- With a population of around 8 million, New York is one of the most densely populated places in the United States.

- New York is famous as America's "melting pot," where immigrants from all over the Old World were welcomed to the New World, landing on Ellis Island beneath the flaming beacon of the Statue of Liberty.

- Of the city's five boroughs, Queens (part of Long Island) has communities of South Americans, Indians, Greeks, Chinese, and Irish.

- The Irish community is particularly strong here, and New York's St. Patrick's Day Parade, or Green Day (17 March), has become one of the major events of the year, when a sea of green marches up Fifth Avenue.

? Yellow taxi cabs are part of the New York scene—and there are an estimated 12,000 of them on call day and night.

historic &
commercial

- When the British took over New Amsterdam in 1664, they renamed it New York City.

- Canals and waterways were dug out in the 18th century, giving better access to the Atlantic and developing New York into a busy seaport.

- Immigration from Europe in the 19th century— including people fleeing the desperate poverty of the potato famine in Ireland—helped fuel a population explosion in the city.

- In 2001 a terrorist attack totally destroyed the twin towers of the World Trade Center, killing an estimated 2,800 people and shocking America to its core.

monuments &
landmarks

- New York's iconic image is the Statue of Liberty, which sits on Liberty Island. A gift from France, it was shipped across the Atlantic in 350 pieces and then reassembled here in 1886.

- The seven rays of the statue's crown represent the seven seas and seven continents of the world.

- The city is synonymous with skyscrapers. The Chrysler Building was the tallest in the world until the Empire State Building took the lead—both are now dwarfed by the modern towers that surround them.

did **you** know?

...it's here?

Washington, DC

THE US FEDERAL CAPITAL, WITH ITS NEO-CLASSICAL BUILDINGS AND DELIBERATELY LOW SKYLINE, IS REGARDED BY MANY AS AMERICA'S MOST ELEGANT CITY.

Q Which famous building is at 1600 Pennsylvania Avenue?

A The White House.

pomp &
circumstance

- Stately Washington, DC, takes its name from George Washington, the first president of the United States, a revolutionary general who was elected to the role in 1789.

- It is still home to the President of the United States and the Federal Government.

- The city's population stands at just over half a million—including an estimated 78,000 lawyers.

- More than 60 percent of the population is black, and Washington's Howard University is the country's oldest African American college.

- Notable structures in the city include the US Capitol Building, the white obelisk of the Washington monument, the Lincoln Memorial, and the Jefferson Monument.

- The temple-like memorials are mirrored by day in the reflecting pool and tidal basin of the Potomac River.

did **you** know?

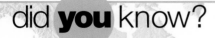

...it's here?

Miami

NICKNAMED THE "AMERIBBEAN," MIAMI IS WHERE FAST FOOD AND MTV AMERICA MEETS SUBTROPICAL CARIBBEAN PALMS AND BANANA PLANTS.

historic &
stylish

- Set where the Miami River channels water from the Florida Everglades into the Atlantic Ocean, the city is named after the Native Indian word for "sweet water."

- Its famous art deco architecture stems from a boom-time in the 1920s and 1930s, when thousands of migrants arrived from the northern states in search of easy fortunes.

- Its proximity to South America has led to big Latin-American companies setting up here.

- Thousands of Cubans who fled Castro's revolution in 1959 came here. Little Havana is a colorful Spanish-speaking, Cuban-American community in the city, alive with salsa music, Cuban cooking, and the craft of cigar-rolling.

Miami *USA*

Q *Where can you see the best of Miami's 800 art deco buildings?*

A *Along Ocean Drive.*

? In 1992 Miami was hit by Hurricane Andrew, which caused 52 deaths and $30 billion worth of damage.

did **you** know?

...it's here?

Havana

HAVANA IS THE SOPHISTICATED CAPITAL OF CUBA, WITH A LIVELY HISTORY, AND A TOURIST INDUSTRY THAT HAS COME OF AGE IN RECENT YEARS.

Q Statues of which man can be found in every settlement across Cuba?

A José Martí (1853–95), the "Father of Cuban Independence."

República de Cuba

culture & **revolution**

- Havana's Old Town, La Habana Vieja, is the oldest, largest, and most impressive historic site in Latin America, with a cathedral dating back to 1748, and a splendid array of museums, churches, bastions, galleries, and memorials.

- The city's best-known structures are its two Spanish-era castles, and the 5-mile (8km) long Malécon, or sea wall.

- The city developed a reputation in the mid-20th century as the seedy and corrupt playground for North Americans, but this was shed after Fidel Castro's successful revolution in 1959.

- Modern Havana has an enviable international reputation as a center for the fine arts, music, and dance.

settlement & **prosperity**

- Spanish settlers founded the city in this spot in 1519, and it soon became the official residence of the Spanish governor—and therefore subject to repeated raids by British privateers.

- By the 18th century Havana had grown to become the third largest city in Latin America.

- The city reached the height of its wealth in the 19th century on the back of the trade in sugar cane, and was made capital of the newly independent Cuba in 1902.

did **you** know?

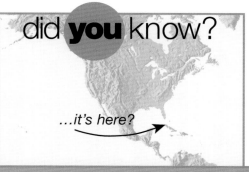

...it's here?

Reykjavík

REYKJAVÍK'S MODERN HARBOR IS HOME TO A STATE-OF-THE-ART TRAWLER FLEET WHICH CONTRIBUTES TO ICELAND'S MOST IMPORTANT INDUSTRY: FISH AND FISH PROCESSING.

facts &
statistics

- Lying at 64.08°N, Reykjavík is the most northerly capital in the world.

- It was named Reykjavík, or "smoky bay," by the First Settler, Norwegian Ingólfur Arnarson, in AD874, after its natural steam vents.

- Reykjavík was declared a city in 1962, and its population stands at around 160,000.

did **you** know?

...it's here?

Ísland

landmarks &
geothermals

- The city's most prominent landmark is the soaring spire of the Hallgrímskirkja, a stark, modern church likened to a rocket awaiting take-off, on Thingholt hill.

- Another notable feature is the space-age Perlan (pearl)—a glass-domed restaurant that sits atop the city's naturally supplied hot water storage tanks.

Q *Which local hero, whose statue stands in front of the Hallgrímskirkja, was the first European to discover America?*

A *Leifur Eiriksson, who sailed there around AD1000.*

157

At midday in Reykjavík it is midnight in Suva and 10pm in Brisbane...   *...do you know where they are?*

Index

A

Acropolis 72
Al-Aqsa Mosque 79
Alcatraz 129
Amsterdam 36-7
Amundsen, Roald 39
Anderson, Hans Christian 40
Apartheid Museum 83
Arc de Triomphe 28
Athens 72-3
Atomium 35
Atwood, Margaret 143
Auckland 122-3
Australia 112-13, 116-21
Austria 58-9
Aztecs 135

B

Bangkok 96-9
Barcelona 26-7
Basilica of St. Mark 47
beer and breweries 35, 45, 55
Beijing 110-11
Belgium 32-5
Berlin 42-3
Blue Mosque 75
Bondi Beach 118
Borodin, Alexander 87
Boston 144-5
Bratislava 60-1
Bruges 32-3
Brussels 34-5
Budapest 66-7
Burj al Arab hotel 91
Burton, Richard 31

C

Cairo 80-1
Canada 124-5, 138-43
Cape Town 84-5
Capone, Al 137

Carnevale 47
Casablanca 22-3
Catherine the Great 87
Charles IV, Emperor 55
Chicago 136-7
China see People's Republic
    of China
Chopin, Frédéric 70
Church of the
    Holy Sepulchre 79
Churchill, Winston 20
CN Tower 142
Colosseum 52
Copenhagen 40-1
Copernicus, Nicolas 69
Croatia 62-5
Cuba 154-5
Czech Republic 54-5

D

Davies, Robertson 143
Delhi 92-3
Denmark 40-1
Doge's Palace 47
Dome of the Rock 79
Dostoyevsky, Fyodor 87
Doyle, Sir Arthur Conan 12
Dubai 90-1
Dublin 10-11
Dubrovnik 62-5

E

Edinburgh 12-13
Edinburgh Festival 12
Egypt 80-1
Eiffel Tower 28
Eiriksson, Leifur 157
Emerald Buddha 99
Empire State Building 149
England 14-15

F

Florence 50-1
Forbidden City 111
Foster, Sir Norman 42
France 28-9
Frank, Anne 36
Franklin, Benjamin 145
Fremantle 112
French Revolution 29

G

Gates, Bill 126
Gaudí, Antonio 27
Germany 42-5
Gogol, Nikolai 87
Golden Gate Bridge 129
Grace, Princess 31
Great Pyramid at Giza 81
Greece 72-3
Greenpeace 122, 125
Guinness Brewery 11

H

Habsburg Empire 58
Harbour Bridge, Sydney 118
Havana 154-5
Hermitage 87
Hillary, Edmund 122
Ho Chi Minh City 100-1
Hofburg 58
Hollywood 130, 131
Hong Kong 106-7
Hungary 66-7

I

Iceland 156-7
India 92-5
Ireland 10-11
Israel 76-9
Istanbul 74-5
Italy 46-53

J

Jama Masjid 92
Japan 114-15
Jerónimos monastery 16
Jerusalem 76-9
Jin Mao Tower 108
Johannesburg 82-3
John Paul II, Pope 69

K

Kaiser Wilhelm
    Memorial Church 42, 43
Kirov Ballet 87
Kolkata (Calcutta) 94-5
Krakow 68-9
Kremlin 88
Kuala Lumpur 102-3

L

lace-making 33
Las Vegas 132-3
Lenin, Vladimir Ilyich 86
Lisbon 16-17
Little Mermaid 40
Ljubljana 56-7
London 14-15
Los Angeles 130-1
Louvre 28
Lutyens, Sir Edwin 93

M

Madrid 24-5
Malaysia 102-3
Malcolm X 144
Mandela, Nelson 85
Manneken-Pis 35
Mao Zedong 111
Maori people 123
Marrakech 18-21
Martí, José 154
Mata Hari 31

Medici family 51
Meiji Shrine 115
Melbourne 120-1
Mexico 134-5
Mexico City 134-5
Miami 152-3
Michelangelo 50, 51
Microsoft 126
Millennium Wheel 14
Monaco 30-1
Mongkut, King 97
Monte Carlo 30-1
Montréal 140-1
Morocco 18-23
Moscow 88-9
Mosque of Hassan II 23
Mozart, Wolfgang
　Amadeus 55, 58, 59
Munich 44-5
Munch, Edvard 39
Murano 47

N
Netherlands 36-7
New York 146-9
New Zealand 122-3
Nobel Peace Prize 39
Norway 38-9

O
Ondaatje, Michael 143
Opera House, Sydney 118
Øresund Bridge 40
Oslo 38-9

P
Parc Güell 27
Paris 28-9
People's Republic
　of China 106-11
Pepys, Samuel 14

Perth 112-13
Peter the Great 87
Petronas Twin Towers 103
Plaza de Toros bullring 25
Plečnik, Jože 56
Poland 68-71
Ponte Vecchio 50
Portugal 16-17
Prague 54-5
Pushkin, Alexander 87

Q
Québec 138-9

R
Raffles Hotel 105
Reclining Buddha 98
Red Fort 92
Reichstag 42, 43
Rembrandt 36, 37
Revere, Paul 145
Reykjavík 156-7
Rijksmuseum 36
Rimsky-Korsakov, Nikolai 87
Robben Island 85
Rome 52-3
Russia 86-9

S
Sagrada Família 27
St. Basil's Cathedral 88
St. Patrick 11, 148
St. Peter's Basilica 52
St. Petersburg 86-7
San Francisco 128-9
Santa Maria del Fiore 50
Scotland 12-13
Scott, Sir Walter 12
Scottish Parliament 12
Seattle 126-7
Shanghai 108-9

Singapore 104-5
Sky Tower 122
Slovakia 60-1
Slovenia 56-7
Soong Ching-ling 108
souks (markets) 21
South Africa 82-5
Space Needle 127
Spain 24-7
Spanish Civil War 27
Stanley Park 125
Statue of Liberty 148, 149
Stevenson, Robert Louis 12
Strauss, Johann 59
Strauss, Richard 44
Sydney 116-19

T
Tagore, Rabindranath 95
Taj Mahal 92
Taylor, Elizabeth 31
Teresa, Mother 95
Thailand 96-9
Tiananmen Square 111
Tintin 35
Tokyo 114-15
Topkapi Palace 75
Toronto 142-3
Trinity College 11
Turkey 74-5
Tutankhamun 81

U
United Arab Emirates 90-1
USA 126-33, 136-7, 144-53

V
Van Gogh Museum 36
Vancouver 124-5
Vasco da Gama bridge 16
Vatican State 52

Venice 46-9
Vienna 58-9
Vietnam 100-1

W
Warsaw 70-1
Washington, DC 150-1
Washington, George 151
Waterloo, Battle of 34
Wenceslas 55
White House 150
Wright, Frank Lloyd 136

Acknowledgments

Abbreviations for terms appearing below: (t) top; (b) bottom; (c) center; (l) left; (r) right; (AA) AA World Travel Library.

The Automobile Association wishes to thank the following photographers and companies for their assistance in the preparation of this book.

3 AA/T Harris; 4c AA/C Sawyer; 4cr AA/P Wood; 5tl AA/R Strange; 5tcl AA/S McBride; 5tc AA/C Sawyer; 5tcr AA/S Day; 5tr AA/P Kenward; 5cl AA/ N Setchfield; 5clc AA/C Sawyer; 5crc AA/A Mockford & N Bonetti; 5cr AA/D Corrance; 8 AA/S McBride; 10b AA/S Day; 10c AA/S Day; 11tr AA/S Whitehorne; 11br AA/S McBride; 12 AA/D Corrance; 12/3 AA/S Whitehorne; 13 AA/M Alexander; 14l AA/S Bates; 14bl AA/C Sawyer; 15 AA/M Jourdan; 15bl AA/P Kenward; 15tr AA/M Jourdan; 16 AA/T Harris; 16/7 AA/A Kouprianoff; 17tr AA/A Kouprianoff; 17c AA/A Mockford & N Bonetti; 18/9 AA/S McBride; 19tr AA/I Burgum; 20t AA/S McBride; 20/1 AA/S McBride; 20b AA/S McBride; 21tr AA/I Burgum; 21c AA/S McBride; 21l AA/S McBride; 22 AA/I Burgum; 23tr AA/I Burgum; 23c AA/I Burgum; 24 AA/M Jourdan; 25l AA/M Jourdan; 25tr AA/M Jourdan; 25cr AA/M Jourdan; 26 AA/S Day; 27tr AA/S Day; 27cr AA/S Day; 27b AA/S Day; 28/9 AA/P Enticknap; 29tr AA/W Voysey; 29r AA/B Rieger; 30/1 AA/A Baker; 31tr AA/C Sawyer; 32 AA/A Kouprianoff; 32/3 AA/A Kouprianoff; 33tr AA/A Kouprianoff; 34cl AA/A Kouprianoff; 34bl AA/A Kouprianoff; 34bc AA/A Kouprianoff; 35 AA/A Kouprianoff; 35tr AA/A Kouprianoff; 36 AA/K Paterson; 37 AA/K Paterson; 37tr AA/K Paterson; 38/9 AA/J Smith; 39tr AA/J Smith; 39c AA/J Smith; 40 AA/D Forss; 41b AA/D Forss; 41tr AA/JW Jorgensen; 42 AA/S McBride; 43tr AA/S McBride; 43bl AA/T Souter; 44 AA/C Sawyer; 45tr AA/M Jourdan; 45cl AA/C Sawyer; 45cr AA/T Souter; 46/7 AA/A Mockford & N Bonetti; 47tr AA/C Sawyer; 48 AA/S McBride; 48/9 AA/A Mockford & N Bonetti; 49tr AA/C Sawyer; 49 AA/S McBride; 50 AA/S McBride; 51l AA/K Paterson; 51tr AA/C Sawyer; 51bc AA/C Sawyer; 52 AA/D Mitidieri; 53 AA/C Sawyer; 53tr AA/S McBride; 54l AA/J Wyand; 54r AA/C Sawyer; 55tr AA/S McBride; 55c AA; 56 Ljubljana Tourist Board/Archive ZTL; 57l Ljubljana Tourist Board/Matjaz Tancic; 57tr Archive Ljubljana Tourist Board; 57bc Ljubljana Tourist Board/B Gradnik; 58 AA/C Sawyer; 58/9 AA/J Smith; 59tr AA; 60 AA/J Smith; 60/1 AA/J Smith; 61tr AA/J Smith; 62/3 AA/P Bennett; 63tr AA/P Bennett; 64 AA/P Bennett; 65l AA/P Bennett; 65tr AA/P Bennett; 65c AA/P Bennett; 66/7 AA/G Wrona; 67tr AA/E Meacher; 68/9 AA/J Smith; 69tr AA/J Smith; 70/1 AA/J Smith; 71tr AA/G Wrona; 73ct AA/P Wilson; 72/3 AA/T Harris; 73tr AA/P Wilson; 73cb AA/R Strange; 74 AA/P Bennett; 75l AA/P Kenward; 75tr AA/D Mitidieri; 76/7 AA/P Aithie; 77tr AA/P Aithie; 78 AA/P Aithie; 79tl AA/P Aithie; 79tc AA/T Souter; 79tr AA/P Aithie; 80 AA/R Strange; 81cr AA/R Strange; 81bl AA/R Strange; 81tr AA/R Strange; 82t South African Tourism; 83bl South African Tourism; 83br South African Tourism; 83tr AA/C Sawyer; 83ct AA/S McBride; 83c South African Tourism; 84 AA/C Sawyer; 85tr AA/P Kenward; 85bl AA/C Sawyer; 86 AA/J Arnold; 87tr AA/K Paterson; 87c AA/K Paterson; 88/9 AA. J Arnold; 89ct AA/K Paterson; 89cb AA/K Paterson; 89tr AA/K Paterson; 90 AA/C Sawyer; 91tr AA/C Sawyer; 91ctr AA/C Sawyer; 91cb AA/C Sawyer; 91ctl AA/C Sawyer; 92r D Corrance; 92br D Corrance; 93tr AA/D Corrance; 93bl AA/D Corrance; 94 AA/F Arvidsson; 95tr AA/F Arvidsson; 95bl AA/F Arvidsson; 95br A/F Arvidsson; 96/7 AA/R Strange; 97tr AA/D Henley; 98t AA/J Holmes; 98b AA/D Henley; 99t AA/J Holmes; 99tr AA/D Henley; 99b AA/J Holmes; 100 AA/D Henley; 101tr AA/D Henley; 101l AA/J Holmes; 101r AA/D Henley; 102 AA/N Setchfield; 103c AA/N Setchfield; 103tr AA/K Paterson; 104/5 AA/N Setchfield; 105 AA/A Kouprianoff; 105c AA/N Setchfield; 106 Kat Mead; 106b Kat Mead; 107tr AA/A Kouprianoff; 107r AA/A Kouprianoff; 108 AA/I Morejohn; 109tr AA/G Clements; 109bl AA/G Clements; 110b AA/G Clements; 110/1 AA/A Kouprianoff; 111tr AA/G Clements; 112 AA/M Langford; 112/3 AA/M Langford; 113tr AA/M Langford; 113c AA/M Langford; 114 AA/J Holmes; 115tr AA/J Holmes; 115cl AA/J Holmes; 115cr A/D Corrance; 116/7 AA/M Langford; 117tr AA/M Langford; 118 AA/M Langford; 119tr AA/M Langford; 119 AA/M Langford; 120/1 AA/B Bachman; 121tr AA/B Bachman; 121bc AA/B Bachman; 122/3 AA/M Langford; 123tr AA/A Belcher; 124cl AA/P Timmermans; 124cr AA/C Sawyer; 125tr AA/C Coe; 125b AA/C Sawyer; 126 AA/J Tims; 127tr Tim Thomson/Seattle's Convention and Visitors Bureau; 127c AA/J Tims; 127bc Tim Thomson/Seattle's Convention and Visitors Bureau; 128 AA/K Paterson; 129tr AA/K Paterson; 129c AA/K Paterson; 130cl AA/M Jourdan; 130b AA/P Wood; 130/1 AA/P Wood; 131tr AA/C Sawyer; 132 AA/L Dunmire; 133tr AA/L Dunmire; 133bl Las Vegas Convention and Visitors Authority; 134 AA/C Sawyer; 135tr AA/C Sawyer; 135c AA/R Strange; 135bc AA/C Sawyer; 136 AA/P Wood; 136/7 AA/P Wood; 137tr AA/P Wood; 137c AA/P Wood; 138 AA/N Sumner; 138/9 AA/J F Pins; 139tr AA/N Sumner; 139c AA/N Sumner; 140 AA/J F Pins; 141tr AA/J F Pins; 141cl AA/J F Pins; 141b AA/J F Pins; 142/3 AA/J F Pins; 143tr AA/J Davison; 144/5 AA/J Nicholson; 145tr AA/J Nicholson; 145b AA/C Sawyer; 146/7 AA/S McBride; 147tr AA/C Sawyer; 148tl AA/S McBride; 148tr AA/S McBride; 148b AA/C Sawyer; 149tl AA/C Sawyer; 147tc AA/C Sawyer; 149tr AA/C Sawyer; 149bc AA/C Sawyer; 149br AA/C Sawyer; 150 AA/E Davies; 151tr AA/C Sawyer; 151c AA/C Sawyer; 151bc AA/C Sawyer; 152/3 AA/P Bennett; 153tr AA/P Bennett; 153bc AA/J Davison; 154 AA/C Sawyer; 155tr AA/D Henley; 155cl AA/C Sawyer; 156br Reykjavik Tourist Information Centre; 157bl Reykjavik Tourist Information Centre; 156/7 Reykjavik Tourist Information Centre; 157tr Reykjavik Tourist Information Centre.

Every effort has been made to trace the copyright holders, and we apologise in advance for any accidental errors. We would be happy to apply the corrections in the following edition of this publication.